THE SECOND COMING OF THE CHURCH

THE
SECOND COMING
OF THE CHURCH

[GEORGE BARNA]

WORD PUBLISHING
Nashville•London•Vancouver•Melbourne

Published in association with Sealy M. Yates,
Literary Agent, Orange, California.

Library of Congress Cataloging-in-Publication Data
Barna, George.
The second coming of the church : a blueprint for survival / George Barna
p.   cm.
Includes bibliographical references.
ISBN 0-8499-1490-6
1. Church renewal—United States. I. Title.
BV600.2.B344   1998
262'.001'7—dc21

Printed in the United States of America
8 9 0 1 2 3 4 BVG 9 8 7 6 5 4

[CONTENTS]

118722

PART III: CHECK OUT THE MAP
A BIBLICAL PERSPECTIVE ON WHAT GOD EXPECTS OF HIS CHURCH

PART IV: REDIRECT THE COURSE
THE CHURCH OF THE FUTURE

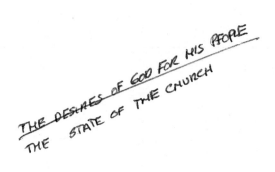

THE ~~DESIRES OF GOD FOR HIS PEOPLE~~

THE   STATE OF THE CHURCH

[PREFACE]

ONE OF THE MOST TROUBLING PASSAGES of Scripture to me is Ecclesiastes 12:12: "Of making many books there is no end." Of the two dozen books I have written, all of them seemed important enough to write. In retrospect, though, a few clearly stand out in my mind as crucial messages for the Church.

A decade ago *The Frog in the Kettle* was meant to be a wake-up call to the Church as it struggled with the concepts of relevance and cultural change. A couple of years later, in *The Power of Vision,* I was privileged to write about the need for every Christian, and especially church leaders, to devote time to understanding the unique mandate God has for each of us who wish to serve Him.[1] In writing such books I distinctly felt that God was using me to communicate a very timely and significant body of information to His Church.

The Second Coming of the Church stands in that same tradition. The first coming of the Church was of course at Pentecost, when the Spirit of God moved among believers and empowered them to pursue the Great Commission, as Jesus commanded. In the New Testament we read of the activities of the early Church and marvel at how quickly the message of the Gospel swept that culture.

In the two thousand years since that time, many great movements of the Spirit have demonstrated God's great faithfulness to His people. And yet, as the second millennium draws to a close, and the Church takes stock of how well we have handled the legacy that was passed down to us, we can't help but wonder . . . and sometimes, to weep.

The last four years of my life have especially been devoted to agonized reflection on the state of the Church, the desires of God for His people, and the growing gap between those two. The result of all that effort is this letter to the Church. It is more personal, more strategic, and more intense than any message I have previously written—and with good reason.

This book is about more than the interplay between the Church and the culture. It is an urgent plea for the people of God to stop dabbling in religion and to grow in spiritual maturity. It is a challenge to ignite and sustain a moral and spiritual revolution in America today, the likes of which we have never seen in our lifetime. This is a call for us to stop *playing* church and start *being* the Church by demonstrating the transformation that has occurred within us as a result of an absolute, paramount commitment to Jesus Christ.

This is a book that goes beyond the debate about the need for change; it is a strategic plan for the rebirthing of the Christian faith in America, drawing from scriptural mandates to determine God's vision for the true Church and what our role is to be in God's kingdom on earth.

America is at a turning point in its history. The decisions we make in the next few years regarding who we are and the values we stand for will seal the moral and spiritual fate of America for decades to come. The decadence and darkness of our nation are more profound than since the founding of this nation more than two centuries ago. The only power that can cleanse and restore this nation is the power of Christ. And the primary way in which that power is to be manifested is by Christ's followers serving God and humanity by being the Church—that is, the true representation of Jesus Christ.

This is our time of testing. We must prove that we are what we claim to be, or we will certainly lose the platform to influence the world for Christ. That privileged position is already slipping from our grasp. Given the moral and spiritual demise of our culture, maintaining that position is not an insignificant challenge. And the sad truth is that the Christian Church, as we now know it, is not geared up to meet that challenge.

Our situation is not hopeless, but it is urgent. Time is of the essence. Godly, strategic leadership, dedicated to the fulfillment of God's vision for America and His Church, is demanded.

If you care about the Church of Christ, please read on, reflect on the content, and act upon it in whatever ways God's Holy Spirit would cause you to respond. Some day God will ask you for an account of how you used the gifts and resources He entrusted to you for His purposes. Use the information outlined within this volume as a tool to become a more effective change agent, for God's glory. The only true purpose for living yet another day is to know, love, and serve God with all your heart, mind, soul, and strength.[2]

May the next few, precious years find us laboring together toward the fulfillment of a common vision that will glorify and honor our Savior.

I wish to gratefully acknowledge the input and support of a myriad of family, friends, and colleagues who sacrificed and contributed so that this book might emerge. My deepest thanks go to my wife (Nancy) and daughters (Samantha and Corban). I am also indebted to Thom Black, Chuck Colson, Leighton Ford, Lee Gessner, Tom Greanias, Bill Greig III, Barry Hawes, Charlie Hedges, Bill Hybels, Kip Jordon, David Kinnaman, Jill Kinnaman, Larry Osborne, Steve Russo, Jim Scott, Molly Scott, Tom Thompson, Pam Tucker, Jim VanYperen, Luder Whitlock, and Sealy Yates for their ideas and encouragement.

[ONE]
THE CHALLENGE: HEALING A DYING BODY

LET'S CUT TO THE CHASE. After nearly two decades of studying Christian churches in America, I'm convinced that the typical church as we know it today has a rapidly expiring shelf life.

Our cultural norms, our personal expectations, and the condition of the Christian community at large have produced a dizzying array of challenges to churches. Across the nation, ministries of all sizes and shapes have responded with a frenzy of religious activity, producing more programs, buildings, events, and resources than would have been imaginable at the turn of the century. Yet, as we prepare to enter into a new century of ministry, we must address one inescapable conclusion: Despite the activity and chutzpah emanating from thousands of congregations, the Church in America is losing influence and adherents faster than any other major institution in the nation. Unless a radical solution for the revival of the Christian Church in the United States is adopted and implemented soon, the spiritual hunger of Americans will either go unmet or be satisfied by other faith groups.

SIGNS OF THE TIMES

Having devoted the last eighteen years of my life to studying the American people, their churches, and the prevailing culture, I've concluded that within the next few years America will experience one of two outcomes: either massive spiritual revival or total moral anarchy.[1] As a committed Christian, I am urgently praying for revival. As a rational social scientist confronted with a warehouse full of behavioral and attitudinal data . . . well, the prospects are not encouraging.

The world around us is changing at an unprecedented pace. What worked ten years ago is already obsolete; cultural analysts estimate that our culture essentially reinvents itself every three to five years. In other words, the core attributes of our society—language, customs, dress styles, dominant leisure pursuits, relational emphases, values, and the like—are being substantially reshaped and reconfigured every few years.

Most American churches, however, are holding fast to programs and goals established by their charter members years ago. Many of these ministries have mastered the art of denying the cataclysmic cultural changes around them, responding with cosmetic changes that make little difference. Is it any wonder that the critical measures of the health of the Christian Church show decline and a loss of influence?

Does this sound like an overstatement? Consider some of the signs of the times. . . .

People are desperate for spiritual truth—but they can't find the answers they need in Christian churches. Studies we have conducted over the past year indicate that a majority of the people who made a first-time "decision" for Christ were no longer connected to a Christian church within just *eight weeks* of having made such a decision! While the evangelistic efforts of some churches and parachurch ministries have garnered positive results, the sad fact is that most of those efforts are wasted because new believers are not being effectively absorbed into a healthy community of believers and, in most cases, never move from "decision" to "conversion."

Ethnic diversity is here to stay, and racial reconciliation is a national concern—but the Church remains our most segregated institution. The Caucasian population is at zero population growth, while the African American, Hispanic, and Asian populations in our country are experiencing double-digit expansion. In fact, by 2050 only half of the nation's population will be Caucasian. The concept of multiculturalism will be increasingly significant in our language, customs, values, relationships, and processes.

Unfortunately, the Church has not kept pace with society. Thirty years after Martin Luther King noted that eleven o'clock on Sunday morning was the most segregated hour of the week, his observation is still accurate. Churches have neither adapted their ministries to serve the needs of different ethnic groups nor demonstrated leadership in eliminating the racial tensions heightened by America's escalating ethnic diversity.

The Church was called by Christ to care for the least of all people, and to be known by the quality of its love. Yet poverty is prospering in America. No nation on earth has a greater net worth than the United States. But that wealth is distributed unequally. The wealthiest 1 percent of the households in America own more than 40 percent of the nation's assets. At the same time, there are more than thirty million Americans who live in poverty—that's more people than live in the entire nations of Canada or Australia! Worse, roughly 40 percent of the poor in America are children. Despite these glaringly apparent needs, churches across the country are minimally involved in addressing this issue. For every dollar spent on ministry to the poor, the typical church spends more than five dollars on buildings and maintenance.

Americans have greater access than ever to advanced education. Yet, increasing numbers of people lack the skills to comprehend God's Word. Nearly half of today's adults are functionally illiterate—that is, they cannot read and write at an eighth-grade level. Consequently, most adults cannot understand the language used in the King James Version of the Bible, which remains the most widely used version in our country. Content analysis of sermons preached in Christian churches indicates that congregations are also unable to comprehend much of the teaching they receive from the pulpit—again, a reflection of flagging literacy. Although Sunday school was originally conceived as a way of teaching people both reading skills and biblical principles, today's churches are doing little to stem the decline in literacy and have failed to adopt new means of effective communication.

Technology and the mass media have forever changed the ways in which we process information. Churches have yet to catch on to the new forms and styles of communication. Young people have grown up under the tutelage of video games, MTV, computers, videos, CD-ROMs, the Internet, and other emerging media. The result is a new mode of thinking in which linear reasoning has been replaced with mosaic thinking, which integrates information and decision making in entirely unique ways. Attention spans have been affected, too: The average attention span among teenagers today is estimated at six to eight minutes. In defiance of these trends, among the most widely used forms of technology in our churches are flannel boards and filmstrip projectors; the average sermon lasts thirty-one minutes and is based upon linear arguments.

AMERICA THE ILLITERATE

- A United States Department of Education study concluded that 54% of American adults are either functionally or marginally literate.

- 60% of United States prison inmates are illiterate.

- 85% of all juvenile offenders have serious problems reading.

- A recent study by the United Nations showed the United States ranked 49th in literacy among the 158 nations evaluated.

- A report by the Department of Labor concluded that 40% of all current jobs require only limited literacy skills, but that only 27% of all newly created jobs also allow for limited literacy.

- Almost half of all adults do not read even one book during a typical year.

- A Barna Research report noted that three-quarters of all adults spent time reading for pleasure during a typical week in 1990. That figure dropped to less than 40% in 1997.

- More than 35 million people in America do not speak English.

- More than one million of last year's high school graduates received their diploma even though they could not read and write at an eighth-grade level.

- The most widely used version of the Bible in the United States is the King James Version (KJV). However, given the literacy skills of the population, slightly more than three out of every four adults are incapable of reading and understanding the KJV due to their literacy limitations.

While America has become the land of the niche market and the home of the specialist, churches are placing excessive demands upon pastors, the ministry generalists. Protestant pastors work an average of nearly sixty-five hours per week, juggling sixteen major dimensions of activity. This torturous pace has made burnout commonplace. The average career span of pastors these days is just half of what it was in 1950. In fact, the average tenure of a pastor in Protestant churches has declined to just four years—even though studies consistently show that pastors experience their most productive and influential ministry in years five through fourteen of their pastorate!

All of these factors taken together paint a grim portrait of America's future—and that of the Christian Church. And it's getting grimmer day by day.

WHERE IS THE CHURCH?

Americans today are more devoted to seeking spiritual enlightenment than at any previous time during the twentieth century. Yet, at this moment of optimum opportunity, Christianity is having less impact on people's perspectives and behaviors than ever. Why is that? Because a growing majority of people have dismissed the Christian faith as weak, outdated, and irrelevant.

Interestingly, the stumbling block for the Church is not its theology but its failure to apply what it believes in compelling ways. The downfall of the Church has not been the content of its message but its failure to practice those truths. Christians have been their own worst enemies when it comes to showing the world what authentic, biblical Christianity looks like—and why it represents a viable alternative to materialism, existentialism, mysticism, and the other doctrines of popular culture.[2] Those who have turned to Christianity and churches seeking truth and meaning have left empty-handed, confused by the apparent inability of Christians themselves to implement the principles they profess. Churches, for the most part, have failed to address the nagging anxieties and deep-seated fears of the people, focusing instead upon outdated or secondary issues and proposing tired or trite solutions.

EXAMPLES OF THE SIMILARITY OF BEHAVIOR
BETWEEN CHRISTIANS AND NON-CHRISTIANS

Behavior	Born-again Christians	Non-Christians
Watch MTV, the music television channel, in the past week	19%	24%^^
Read all or part of a book for pleasure, in the past week	50%	57%^^
Registered to vote	83%	79%**
Donated any money to a nonprofit organization, in past month	47%	48%**
Have been divorced (among those who have been married)	27%	23%^^
Volunteered time to help a nonprofit organization, in past week	29%	27%**
Had a discussion with someone about politics, in past week	41%	47%^
Bought a lottery ticket, in the past week	23%	27%**
Took part in exercise or athletic activity, in past week	59%	63%**
Intentionally encouraged or complimented someone, in past week	86%	77%**
Gave money to a homeless person or poor person, in past year	24%	34%"
Work from your home (full-time or part-time)	29%	35%"
Subscribe to cable television	70%	70%"
Contacted a public official to express your opinion, in past year	41%	40%"
Attended a community meeting on local issue, in past year	37%	42%"
Had a session with a professional counselor, in past year	15%	15%"
Returned a product you were dissatisfied with, in past year	70%	73%"
Filed a lawsuit against someone, in past year	3%	4%"
Took drugs or medication prescribed for depression, in past year	7%	8%"
Participated in a chat room on the Internet, in past year	8%	11%"
Participated in a boycott or public demonstration, in past year	7%	10%"
Tried to influence someone's opinion on an issue, in past year	47%	49%"
Sent letter to a company protesting their ethics, in past year	9%	10%"
Watched a PG-13 or R-rated movie, in past 3 months	76%	87%"
Watched an X-rated movie in the past 3 months	9%	16%"

Sources:
* OmniPoll 2-97, July 1997, N=1012, Barna Research Group, Ltd., Oxnard, CA.
** OmniPoll 1-97, January 1997, N=1007, Barna Research Group, Ltd., Oxnard, CA.
^ OmniPoll 2-96, July 1996, N=1018, Barna Research Group, Ltd., Oxnard, CA.
^^ OmniPoll 1-96, January 1996, N=1004, Barna Research Group, Ltd., Oxnard, CA.
" Donor Compass 97-2, August 1997, N=1087, Barna Research Group, Ltd., Oxnard, CA.

The profound practical irrelevance of Christian teaching, combined with the lack of perceived value associated with Christian church life, has resulted in a burgeoning synthetic faith. Having been exposed to basic Christian principles at various times in their lives, and perceiving all truth to be relative to the individual and his or her circumstances, Americans have taken to piecing together a customized version of faith that borrows liberally from any available and appealing faith.

Consider how we have repositioned spirituality. Faith used to revolve around God and His ordinances and principles; the faith that arrests our attention these days is that which revolves around us. We have demystified God, befriended Jesus, abandoned the Holy Spirit, and forgiven and even warmed up to Satan. Few Americans possess a sense of awe, fear, or trembling related to God.

To increasing millions of Americans, God—if we even believe in a suprahuman deity—exists for the pleasure of humankind. He resides in the heavenly realm solely for our utility and benefit. Although we are too clever to voice it, we live by the notion that true power is accessed not by looking upward but by turning inward. The focus of our faith has shifted from the transcendent to the mundane.

Most Christians—not those who merely call themselves Christians but those who have confessed their sinfulness and have asked Jesus Christ to be their Lord and Savior—have fallen prey to the same disease as their worldly counterparts. We think and behave no differently from anyone else.[3] This problem is compounded by the fact that the individuals in positions of Christian leadership generally do an inadequate job of leading God's people. The systems, structures, institutions, and relational networks developed for the furtherance of the Church are archaic, inefficient, and ineffective—and, perhaps, even unbiblical.

Our problem, then, is not theological but practical in nature: How can we get Christians, who corporately constitute the Church, to be the light in the darkness by living out core biblical principles and creating a better earthly existence for all of humankind?

NO MORE INCREMENTALISM

A serious condition calls for a serious remedy. The time for study commissions and ecumenical debates is past. Merely tinkering with processes and structures will not do. Praying for better times is a necessary but insufficient tonic. Where a dose of strong medicine may have healed some of our infirmities in the past, we now require major reconstructive surgery if we are to move beyond reliance upon life-support systems.

Our goal cannot simply be a timid, powerless survival; it must be the role that Christ called the Church to play, that of a loving, authoritative, healing, and compelling influence upon the world. What we need is true spiritual renewal—a transformation that goes well beyond mere evangelistic outreach. We desperately need a holistic revolution of mind, heart, and spirit. Lacking such a turnabout, we may rightfully anticipate the virtual disappearance of the Christian Church in this nation.

At the risk of sounding like an alarmist, I believe the Church in America has no more than five years—perhaps even less—to turn itself around and begin to affect the culture, rather than be affected by it. Because our culture completely reinvents itself every three to five years, and people are intensely seeking spiritual direction, and our central moral and spiritual trends are engulfed in a downward spiral, we have no more than a half-decade to turn things around.

Before we can hope to do so, though, we must rekindle our passion for God, recapture a sense of urgency about ministry, and respond strategically to the challenges before us. If the Church does not quickly realign its heart, mind, and soul, and consequently redirect its efforts, we will lose our waning platform of influence in American society and people will consistently pursue the path of least moral resistance. Moral anarchy will reign: There will be no rules, laws, traditions, customs, or other parameters that will shape our culture consistently and favorably. It will be every man for himself, with no second thoughts or regrets about the personal or societal implications of this incredibly selfish, nihilistic, narcissistic way of life.

Fortunately, there is hope. If we take strong measures immediately, the people of God may still, by God's grace, emerge to become the mighty Church of Christ. In order for this to happen, however, we must respond strategically—and pray like we've never prayed before.

TURNING THE SHIP AROUND

A popular analogy to the challenge of changing institutions relates to the process of turning an oil tanker around. Although these mammoth ships move relatively slowly and operate in open waters, it takes more than one mile for them to pull a U-turn.

If we are serious about strengthening the Church, then we must redirect its efforts. The time and resources consumed in the turnaround process demand that we initiate this process immediately or, like an oil tanker that suddenly discovers an obstruction in its charted path, we may run aground before we know what hit us.

To outline how I will approach the Church's turnaround process in this book, let's continue the seafaring analogy. First, to facilitate a successful journey, an experienced captain will conduct an exhaustive examination of his ship to ensure that she is seaworthy, and he will repair any damage that might undermine the voyage. Next, after carefully checking the boat, the captain will scrutinize nautical charts and current weather maps. Armed with data, he will then chart a course to maximize safety and efficiency. Then, before leaving port, the captain will review appropriate plans, practices, and parameters with the crew. Finally, once the journey is under way, the captain will constantly examine new information regarding the journey in progress to make any necessary adjustments to the original plan. These course corrections are imperative to ensure a successful voyage.

This book will approach the spiritual journey of the Christian Church in America along the same lines of action. In Part I, we will evaluate "our ship"—that is, the state of the Church and the faith culture in America today. Part II will focus upon the "navigational environment"—for example, the cultural context in which the Church operates. Those chapters will address trends in demographics, attitudes, values, beliefs, and lifestyles that relate to the health and purposes of the Church.

Before we leave the port, though, we must be reminded of our fundamentals—namely, the foundational elements that limit, direct, and shape our ministry purposes and efforts. The chapters in Part III will therefore describe the biblical exhortations regarding the life and functions of churches and the Church; the necessity of effective leadership within the Church; and the centrality of believers possessing and operating in concert with a biblical worldview.

Finally, in Part IV, we will discuss the adjustments we must make to ensure that the Church in America is healthy, functional, and biblical. This discussion will touch on the three keys to redirecting our course as well as the role of the family in the spiritual renewal of the Church. We will close with a discussion of what a revolutionary journey of this nature might look like after all is said and done.

BUCKLE UP!

Jesus once taught His followers that if they knew the truth, the truth would set them free.[5] This has become a treasured principle to me: Always seek the truth and act upon it strategically. Dealing with the truth can lead to victory; being blinded by deceptions can only lead to defeat.

But during my spiritual journey I have also discovered a corollary principle: The truth may set you free, but the truth is not always pleasant to acknowledge or address.

As we study the Church, our culture, and our future, we will likely tap into some truths and revelations that are not easy for you to accept or confront. Meaningful change is never easy; truth is sometimes harsh. Nothing said in these pages regarding people, churches, or our nation is shared for shock value; these matters are shared because I love the Church and long for God's people to experience the joy and freedom accessible through faith in Christ and to exercise appropriate influence in the lives of other people.

To some, the message will sound severe. But these are words that *must* be said if we are to face reality and prepare the Church of Jesus Christ for obedience, growth, and impact in the days to come. I would not have bothered to write this volume of challenges if I did not believe that the Church matters to Christ Himself, that the Church is worth fighting for, and that the Christian Church in America can be resuscitated. And as difficult as it may be to hear these words and think about changing—radically, in some cases— the alternative is worse: to continue doing what we have been doing, the way we have been doing it, and being an accessory to the moral and spiritual disintegration of America.

If you and I commit to openly and intelligently addressing the realities described in this book, the result is likely to be nothing less than the explosive, world-changing revitalization of the Christian Church in America. We serve a God who loves us so much that He allowed His only Son to be sacrificed on our behalf.[6] We serve a God who promises us that He will never leave us or forsake us, a God who assures us that the enemy will not win the war.[7] Through our faith in Christ, and His in us, there is always hope.

[TWO]
CHRISTIANITY GETS A MAKEOVER

As we prepare to bring the Church into the next century, we need to step back and assess our current situation. How effective have we been in living out our Christian faith? How well have we been doing in reaching others with the life-transforming message of the gospel? Is there any room for improvement?

A GLIMPSE INSIDE THE AVERAGE AMERICAN CHURCH

In a very real sense, there is no such thing as an *average* or *typical* church in America. The 340,000 Christian churches in our nation run the gamut from tiny congregations of less than twenty people to megachurches attracting more than fifteen thousand people every weekend. Other churches meet in rented gymnasiums, public schools, people's homes, office buildings, shopping centers, and a variety of church campuses. Several thousand churches are pastored by individuals who have full-time, non-ministry jobs during the week; they pastor as a labor of love and out of an irresistible sense of calling. Other churches have more than two hundred people on their payrolls to oversee the multifaceted operations of their church. Numerous churches offer a single weekend worship service and nothing else; tens of thousands of other churches offer a smorgasbord of programs, classes, and events designed to meet the needs of a wide array of people.

Our research among churches suggests that there are perhaps three dominant classes of churches. The first is the small churches that focus on the needs of people living near the church. These ministries generally have fewer than one hundred people involved and struggle to figure out how to attract young people and families. Their congregational profile tends to be retired Caucasians who have been in their church for several decades. These ministries attract few visitors, and a large proportion of those who visit never return. Those who are regulars appreciate the intimacy and the close relationships they have built within their church.

The small churches tend to offer a Sunday morning worship time, complete with organ and hymns; a Sunday evening service, attended by a handful of the faithful; and perhaps a midweek evening service, designed for in-depth Bible teaching. There is often a midweek daytime Bible study taught by the pastor and attended by a few of the older women in the body. Additional programs are limited in number and nature; those that exist reflect the advanced age of most members (for example, hospital visitation, bingo, women's service circle).

The elders of the nation's small churches are just that: elderly, longtime members who have typically served on the governing board for many years. Change of any type comes slowly to these churches. They are proud of their history and see great value in continuing the traditions on which their church was founded. The facility in which they meet, a modern and attractive structure when it was first built many decades ago, now looks tired and worn. The pastor's constant challenge is not only to encourage his slowly dissipating flock but also to imagine creative ways of bringing new life into the church. Such churches represent half of all Protestant churches in the United States.

The second class of churches is those that are slightly larger, attracting an average of two hundred to four hundred people each weekend. One out of every four Protestant churches fits this category. These churches appeal to young families and have a wider range of congregational activities, ranging from peer groups for mothers of preschoolers to young adult basketball leagues to divorce recovery groups. The church's building is used throughout the week for various purposes, mostly ministry activities focused on the needs of church members. These churches are more aggressive evangelistically, sponsoring one or two community events each year to invite unchurched people to experience what their church has to offer. A primary goal of these churches is numerical growth, which will enable them to expand their range of programs and to expand their facilities.

The lay leaders of these churches represent a mixture of young and old, white collar and blue collar, long-term members, and relative newcomers. It is this blend of divergent backgrounds that introduces vitality into the church's decision-making processes. The pastor, too, is usually in his mid-thirties to mid-fifties—young enough to push the people to dream newer and bigger dreams yet experienced enough to orchestrate an effective team effort to implement those ideas. One of the pastor's consistent challenges is to keep people focused on the vision and primary goals of the church, allocating the ministry's resources for maximum impact. At its current size, these congregations are often just shy of achieving critical mass as they seek to expand their roster of ministries and programs.

The third class of churches consists of the large congregations that dot our landscape. Although they get the lion's share of media attention, they represent just a fraction of the aggregate church world. (For instance, churches that attract one thousand or more people to services in a typical weekend—and are thus classified as "megachurches"—constitute less then 3 percent of all of our nation's churches.) These are the churches noted for their comprehensive menu of activities, programs, and events. They strive to have something for everybody and work hard at being sensitive to the needs and expectations of visitors. Their facilities are in constant use, serving an unusual mixture of people from the church, people from other churches, and those who have no church affiliation but appreciate the ministry and social services offered.

Demographically, these congregations are often a mirror image of the profile of the community at-large. More often than not, these churches are less than forty years old and blossomed by attracting Baby Boomers. Consequently, these churches have a Boomer feel to them—the music, the architecture, the management style, and so forth. The pastors of these churches are typically Boomers, too. The lay leaders are generally an upscale lot: well-educated, professional, upwardly mobile. They take their cues from the senior pastor and are not afraid to take risks. Not surprisingly, the majority of these churches are located in suburban areas.

Naturally, thousands of churches fall in between these categories. But the three types described represent the majority (some 76 percent) and the most common stereotypes. Despite the public ferment about the changing religious environment in the nation, the church world has changed relatively little in the last half century. As always, there are new formats, new structures, and new superstars that arrest the public's attention, but when all factors are objectively assessed, the picture looks pretty much the same as usual: mostly small congregations involved in an unchanging set of programs and events designed to satisfy a well-defined, consistent group of needs relative to a rather circumscribed group of people.

The Way We Express Our Faith Is Changing

People are spending more time involved in religious activities, and spending more money on religious products and services, than at any time in the past fifty years. However, there are a number of trends in the way people practice their faith that must be considered before we can accurately assess the overall health of the Church today.

Church attendance. Overall attendance at Christian churches has slumped somewhat; people are going less regularly, and are becoming more selective. Worship remains an art that most people have tried—and tens of millions continue to invest in each week. However, nearly one-fifth of all churchgoers now attend more than one church, usually on a rotating basis, in order to meet their spiritual needs and satisfy their theological curiosity.

Small groups (cell groups) never really seem to have caught on; fewer than one out of every five adults is presently active in one. Sunday school remains an activity reserved primarily for the children of churched people.

Personal Scripture study. Fewer people are reading the Bible these days (one-third do so in a typical week), largely because we are less inclined to read and fewer people believe that the Bible is an accurate representation of truth.

Church commitments. While people are deeply interested in faith and seeking a more intense connection to God, they are apparently too busy to devote much time to their search for meaning.

Twenty years ago, those most committed to their churches averaged four blocks of time during the week to corporate religious activities; today, the most committed church people allocate two blocks per week. With one of those blocks typically being the Sunday morning worship service, that leaves only one other segment of their weekly calendar open to church-related activities.

Community building. Because of this decline in weekly interaction, building a sense of community within a church has become one of its greatest challenges. People are anxious to make and maintain friendships, and the church has emerged as one of the few places left where they can do so. However, the potential for developing a network of church-based relationships is undermined by the lack of time people devote to church activities, their poor relational skills, and their disinterest in establishing a deeper commitment to the churches they attend.

From "Church Home" to "Spiritual Pit Stop"

Our inability to cultivate lasting communities of faith is partly a result of changes we have made to the church infrastructure, and partly a result of changing perspectives that people embrace toward their faith experience.

More and more Americans are beginning to view churches as a "rest stop" along their spiritual journey, rather than as their final destination. This is fueled by four main factors:

- our transience—15 to 20 percent of all households relocate each year;

- our preference for variety in our church experiences, rather than getting the most out of all that a single church has to offer;

- our perception that spiritual enlightenment comes from diligence in a discovery process, rather than commitment to a faith group and perspective; and

- our repositioning of religion as a commodity that we consume, rather than one in which we invest ourselves.

This detachment takes a toll on the spiritual life of individuals. The tenuous connection many people have to their faith community makes most Americans unwilling to be held accountable for their beliefs and their resulting behaviors. Less than one out of every seven adults is currently in any type of serious spiritual accountability relationship, and there are even fewer others who are anxious to enter into such a relationship.

Similarly, the demands of ministry outreach appeal to relatively few because most Americans view religion as a source of strength you draw from, not a reservoir of positive impact that you must also invest in. The prevailing wisdom is that matters of faith are a take-only, not a give-and-take proposition.

In the end, the Church must address the contradiction between what the Bible exhorts us to pursue spiritually and what Americans have chosen to pursue, based upon cultural assumptions and preferences.

The Bible instructs us to approach God with fear and trembling, befitting our awe at His majesty and love, focusing on who He is, what He has done, and what He expects of us; the culture encourages us to treat God as an equity partner focused on our personal development.

Scripture mandates that we seek and embrace God's truth; our culture exhorts us to achieve refreshment through variety of experience.

True Christianity is about a vertical relationship with God, first and foremost, and allowing that relationship to shape our relationships with others. The American perspective, however, places the emphasis upon our horizontal relationships; interaction with God is simply perceived as a "bonus."

The financial picture is affected, too. People's participation in global missions is waning. While many Americans have adopted a global mind-set within the past decade, American Christians are increasingly devoted to domestic ministry and causes to the exclusion of international ministry opportunities.

Our research on people's giving habits bears out this shift. Even though we continue to give massive sums of money to religious activity, the share assigned to overseas ministry is in decline. As a skeptical people, we like to have tangible evidence of how our donations are being used to further the causes we support.[1]

Our Belief System Is Changing, Too

Most Americans have at least an intellectual assent when it comes to God, Jesus Christ, and angels. They believe that the Bible is a good book filled with important stories and lessons. And they believe that religion is very important in their lives.

But this same group of people, including many professing Christians, also believe that people are inherently good; that our primary purpose is to enjoy life as much as possible; that the primary importance of Christmas Day is our ability to spend time with family; and that our most important responsibility is to take care of family.

STREET-LEVEL THEOLOGY:
WHAT AMERICANS REALLY BELIEVE

American view: The Bible teaches that God helps those who help themselves. (81%^^)
Bible view: We are helpless; we must rely completely upon God. (Ps. 37:39–30)

American view: It doesn't matter what religious faith you follow because they all teach the same lessons. (38%^)
Bible view: Jesus, alone is the Savior of humankind. (Rev. 1:8; 15:4)

American view: All people will experience the same outcome after death, regardless of their religious beliefs. (44%^)
Bible view: Only those who believe in Christ will be saved. (Rom. 3:21–26)

American view: The Bible teaches that money is the root of all evil. (49%")
Bible view: Love of money is the root of many evil pursuits. (1 Tim. 6:10)

American view: People are blessed by God so they can enjoy life as much as possible. (72%^)
Bible view: People are blessed to be a blessing to others. (Gen. 12:1–3)

American view: The most important task in life is taking care of family. (56%^)
Bible view: The most important task is to love God with all our heart, soul, mind and strength. (Matt. 22:37)

American view: The primary purpose of life is enjoyment and fulfillment. (58%)
Bible view: Primary purpose of life is to love God completely. (Deut. 6:5)

American view: The Bible is not totally accurate in all that it teaches. (34%*)
Bible view: All Scripture is from God and therefore is true and reliable. (2 Tim. 3:16)

American view: All religious faiths teach equally valid truths. (40%")
Bible view: Accepting Jesus is the only way to receive salvation. (John 14:6)

American view: All people pray to the same god or spirit, no matter what name they use for that spiritual being. (53%")
Bible view: There is only one God who can justify people. (Rom. 3:30)

American view: Satan is not a living being but is just a symbol of evil. (60%*)
Bible view: Satan is real, powerful, and evil. (1 Peter 5:8)

American view: If a person is generally good or does enough good things for others during their life, they will earn a place in heaven. (55%*)
Bible view: No one is righteous in God's eyes; salvation is by grace alone. (Rom. 3:10; Matt. 19:16–30; Acts 4:12)

American view: When He lived on earth, Jesus Christ committed sins. (44%*)
Bible view: Jesus is divine; He never commited a sin, although He bore all the sins of humankind. (2 Cor. 5:21)

American view: The Holy Spirit is not a living entity but just a symbol of God's power or presence. (61%**)
Bible view: The Spirit dwells within the hearts of all true believers. (2 Cor. 1:22)

American view: After He was crucified, Jesus Christ did not return to life physically. (40%**)
Bible view: He was resurrected, spent time with His followers, then returned to heaven. (Acts 1:1–9; John 20–21)

American view: Whatever works in your life is the only truth you can know. (32%**)
Bible view: God's truth is made clear through the Bible and the Holy Spirit. (John 8:32; Heb. 4:12; 1 Cor. 2:10–16)

American view: There are some sins that not even God can forgive. (34%^^)
Bible view: God can forgive any sin if we truly repent. (1 John 1:9)

Sources:
* OmniPoll 2-97, July 1997, N=1012, Barna Research Group, Ltd., Oxnard, CA.
** OmniPoll 1-97, January 1997, N=1007, Barna Research Group, Ltd., Oxnard, CA.
^ OmniPoll 2-96, July 1996, N=1018, Barna Research Group, Ltd., Oxnard, CA.
^^ OmniPoll 1-96, January 1996, N=1004, Barna Research Group, Ltd., Oxnard, CA.
" OmniPoll 2-94, July 1994, N=1015, Barna Research Group, Ltd., Oxnard, CA.

Worse, 61 percent say there is no such thing as the Holy Spirit; about the same number say there is no such thing as Satan. Nearly half of the population believes that when Jesus Christ was on earth He committed sins! Four out of every ten adults contend that Jesus died on a cross but that He never had a physical resurrection, only a spiritual renaissance.

The most quoted "Bible verse" in America is: "God helps those who help themselves"; 82 percent believe that is a direct quote from the Bible. If you examine the content of that passage—which was originally penned by Thomas Jefferson—it perfectly summarizes American theology. In essence, it teaches that we must make things happen on the strength of our own abilities and efforts, and when we prove ourselves capable or succeed in achieving our goals, then God is obligated to bless us.

Even the issue of salvation has been obfuscated by religious rhetoric. Most adults have heard the distinction between grace-based and works-based salvation; however, most people consider it an either-or proposition, and have already chosen their preference, believing that they have adequately covered themselves for eternity. However, well less than half of all adults have chosen to rely upon Christ as their mediator come the Day of Judgment; most Americans persist in relying upon their good works and good intentions.[2]

What this amounts to is a nation hooked on syncretism—the blending of a variety of perspectives into an entirely new and heretical mixture of faith views—which is then called Christianity even though it bears little resemblance to the faith conveyed in the Bible.

Although most Americans believe they already know the fundamental truths of the Scriptures, our research has discovered that fewer than 10 percent of American *Christians* actually possess a biblical worldview, a perceptual filter through which they see life and its opportunities. Lacking that filter, most Christians make important decisions on the basis of instinct, emotion, assumptions, past experience, external pressure, or chance.

In essence, while millions of Americans possess beliefs that qualify them as Christian, assert that the Bible contains practical lessons and principles for life, and claim that they believe God wants to bless their efforts, they ignore their spiritual resources when the rubber meets the road.

In short, the spirituality of Americans is Christian in name only. We desire experience more than knowledge. We prefer choices to absolutes. We embrace preferences rather than truths. We seek comfort rather than growth. Faith must come on our terms or we reject it. We have enthroned ourselves as the final arbiters of righteousness, the ultimate rulers of our own experience and destiny. We are the Pharisees of the new millennium.

HOW CAN WE BEGIN TO BRING WHOLENESS TO THE CHURCH?

If we are ever going to be an effective and positive influence in American society, we must begin by taking steps to restore the Church—and all those within the Church—to spiritual wholeness. In order to do that, we must first look at how we have failed, both individually and corporately, so that we might learn from the past in order to correct our course.

One mark of a champion is the habit of quickly learning lessons from failures, resulting in a new and improved behavior. Successful people make mistakes, but they achieve success because they rarely make the same mistake twice; every experience is a learning experience to them. Thomas Edison, Abraham Lincoln, Walt Disney, and Brian Tracy are just a few well-known winners who encountered failure after failure but refused to give up. Instead they studied their failures and used them as stepping-stones to victory.

Recent research shows that this same developmental capacity characterizes growing organizations. It is impossible for any organization to avoid miscues. Management consultant Peter Senge, in his classic book on systems thinking and learning organizations, describes this diligence at overcoming setbacks a commitment to truth. It requires "a relentless willingness to root out the ways we limit or deceive ourselves from seeing what is, and to continually challenge our theories of why they are. It means continually broadening our awareness."[3] Success is a result of building on the lessons emerging from our experience.

As we prepare to discuss the second coming of the Church, it is important for us to identify the lessons to be gleaned from our missteps and experiments of the recent past. Rather than disassociate ourselves from our failures, we may embrace them as educational tools that enable us to construct a more responsive and satisfying model for the future. We have paid dearly for those mistakes; let's not multiply the cost by ignoring the lessons and repeating our foibles. Building a strong foundation is a mixture of utilizing proven strengths, avoiding past failures, and devising innovative and strategic solutions to remaining dilemmas.

Toward that end, then, let's specify what our past has taught us. One of the failures that has most hampered effective ministry is the fact that we have been operating under assumptions that, when examined, are unsupported.

One of the first lessons that we must take to heart is:

BAD ASSUMPTIONS WILL KILL YOUR MINISTRY

Many of the failures that have hampered the Church have been the result of bad assumptions. In some cases we have created ministry disasters because we acted on the basis of assumptions we did not even know we embraced. In other cases our actions failed not because we were oblivious to our foundational assumptions, but because those assumptions were simply inaccurate. Untested assumptions will often come back to haunt you.

Here is a listing of just a few of the fundamental assumptions that have harmed the progress or health of the American church within the past two decades.

ASSUMPTION:

Americans have a firm understanding of the basic tenets of Christianity.

The research shows just the opposite: Although more than four out of five people say they have a good comprehension of basic Christian teachings and principles, less than one out of ten are able to correctly identify what the New Testament teaches regarding fundamental principles that relate to their life.

The Bible knowledge of most Americans is astoundingly limited. In fact, most Americans cannot identify any specific beliefs or attributes that distinguish Christianity from other major world religions. If we build the Church on the assumption that we are expanding a viable, preexisting base of knowledge, rather than operating as if no such base exists, the Church will suffer.

ASSUMPTION:

People who believe in God believe in the God of Israel.

Since more than nine out of ten Americans own at least one Bible, and 86 percent call themselves Christian, you might expect people to pay homage to the deity described and followed by the Christian Church. In July 1997, we asked a nationwide sample of 1,012 adults to describe the God they believe in. Two out of three adults (67 percent) said they believe that God is the all-knowing, all-powerful Creator of the universe who rules the world today. The remaining one-third described their god as "the total realization of personal, human potential"; or "a state of higher consciousness that a person may reach"; or said, "Everyone is God"; "There are many gods, each with different power and authority"; or "There is no such thing as God." The remaining 5 percent said they did not know.

Assuming that people are referring to the God of Israel when they refer to their deity of choice could certainly result in confusion, frustration, and an unreliable community of faith. It may also result in missed opportunities to truly inform and challenge people to embrace true Christian faith.

ASSUMPTION:
If a pastor is a good enough teacher,
that gift will compensate for mediocre leadership.

People need to be taught the truths of Scripture; the teaching gift is greatly needed in the Church today. But teaching cannot compensate for a lack of effective leadership.

Americans desperately need to be led. Assuming that decent teaching without good leadership can adequately direct people's spiritual paths and personal lives is the recipe for disaster that has permitted the Church to lose its influence and impact.

ASSUMPTION:
It's okay for the congregation
not to bring the Bible to church services.

In the 1970s, "seeker churches" made a strong theoretical argument for the importance of encouraging people to feel no obligation to tote a Bible to church. Their goal was to make visitors feel welcome and comfortable by alleviating the need to locate a Bible, by diminishing the stressful expectation that they will have to use that Bible during the church service, and by softening the negative image that may be associated with a Bible-toting congregation.

Two decades later, it is clear that this experiment had a more sinister consequence; people don't even know where their Bibles are anymore! In many churches, the core membership—not just the visitors for whom the tactic was originally embraced—began to lose its familiarity with the Bible. There has been a trade-off; changing the rules to help some has impaired the spiritual health of others. Sadly, the shift away from promoting the personal responsibility to bring along a Bible has sent a signal to many people that the Bible is not important.

As the Church has abandoned the Bible, knowledge of scriptural content has declined, personal Bible reading has declined, the image of the Bible as sacred literature has declined, and the ability of people to comprehend biblical principles has declined. In fact, when it comes time to discuss what the Church ought to be, biblical exhortations do not even enter the discussion.

ASSUMPTION:

A qualified pastor should have a seminary degree.

The built-in assumption, of course, is that seminaries recruit godly people who are called to full-time ministry service and possess great leadership potential, then train them to be competent church leaders, awarding the degree as a credential of fitness to lead people in their spiritual journey.

In reality, seminaries do nothing of the kind. They remove seminarians from the real world for several years and put them through an academic exercise in which they are taught how to exegete Scripture and teach. Those are important and necessary skills for the Church, but they are not synonymous with leadership. Consequently, both churches and pastors are set up for failure and disappointment.

ASSUMPTION:

The best way to revitalize churches is to create new ones.

Protestant denominations are aggressively pursuing this tactic, with more than thirty thousand new churches planned to be launched in the nineties alone!

Unfortunately, most of the churches begun have been doomed from the get-go. Typically they launch with the wrong individual in charge (pastors who are not the catalytic, entrepreneurial leaders required), with an inadequate core group (based on the number and nature of the people involved), an outdated model, and severe undercapitalization.

As a rule of thumb it takes roughly a quarter of a million dollars to launch a healthy church using the standard congregational model. Few churches have that kind of start-up cash available. And as with most new businesses, if they are undercapitalized from the start, their chances of success are minimal. Add the wrong leader and an inadequate core group and disaster ensues.

ASSUMPTION:
Non-Christians are vitally interested in salvation.

Christians generally believe that non-Christians are interested in talking to us about eternal security. In truth, most non-Christians don't care to discuss the matter because they believe they already have their eternal security sewn up. A majority of Americans believe they are going to heaven after they die; most of the people who are not relying on Christ's atonement for their sins are relying instead on their own good deeds, their good character, or the generosity of God. Research indicates that the evangelistic efforts of Christians are viewed as insensitive and unnecessary.

The list of deadly assumptions is virtually endless, but you get the point. If the Church of tomorrow is going to be healthy and growing, rather than confused and in retreat, we must question all assumptions. Questioning what we do, who we are, how we minister, and what we stand for is not a hallmark of fear and weakness; it is a sign of wisdom, courage, and hope.

Now that we have taken a closer look at some of the false assumptions that have caused many churches to lose their effectiveness, let's take this a step farther. In the next two chapters we will examine every church's single greatest resource—its people. Specifically, we will explore the dynamics taking place in the congregations of the nineties, and the ministry realities of those who are trying to lead them.

[THREE]
IN SEARCH OF LEADERSHIP

BEING A PASTOR THESE DAYS may be the single most thankless task in America. National surveys indicate that people are less likely to trust and to be influenced by clergy than used to be the case, and that pastors themselves are increasingly frustrated in ministry. Nevertheless, millions of Americans turn to churches for spiritual, emotional, and material help; what they receive is largely dependent upon the leadership pastors exert within their churches. As our culture becomes more complex, and people's needs become more challenging, the quality of pastoral leadership is one of the most significant indicators of the current health and potential inflluence of the Church in America.

A PASTOR'S VIEW OF THE CHURCH

"Well, it's certainly not what I expected, but you work with what you're given."

That's how Paul Corrales, senior pastor of a midsize, nondenominational congregation in the West describes his experience. He served as youth pastor, associate pastor, and interim pastor in denominational churches before accepting a call four years ago to lead his present church. Now, he says, he works "without a safety net."

"We're an independent congregation," he observes, "with all the pluses and minuses that brings with it. I can't imagine doing anything that has greater meaning. Think about it: I get to spend my life introducing people to Jesus Christ, facilitating worshipful experiences with God, encouraging people to mature in their faith, and providing the resources required for that growth."

Now forty-six years old, he entered ministry after spending a few years working in secular jobs. "After I graduated from college I had no clue who I was or what I wanted to do. Then, through a series of unlikely events, I came to recognize my need for Christ. I turned my life over to Him, and it wasn't long before I realized that devoting my life to serving Him would be the ultimate kick. I spent a year or two working through the possibilities with pastors and other godly people from my church before I felt comfortable that full-time ministry was right for me."

In spite of his appreciation for his chosen career, Paul is very up front about the joys and disappointments of pastoral ministry, and how frustrated he has been by the lack of preparation he received from his three years in seminary. "The highs in ministry can be exhilarating, but the lows can be very deep. There are days when I believe that if I knew then what I know now about churches and people and the pastorate, I definitely would not have pursued a full-time ministry career.

"But perhaps God in His wisdom protected me from these insights. This is where He wants me, so maybe He kept me in the dark, knowing that my own inclination would have been to avoid the difficulties inherent in this career. In fact, it was only recently that I have come to grips with the fact that the Lord gave me the spiritual gift of teaching, yet I spend most of my time operating in areas that have nothing to do with that gift."

Like so many of his colleagues across America, Paul believes that there is great danger in the local church changing too rapidly—just as serious harm can result when churches refuse to keep pace with society. He sees the church as a place where people ought to be able to be themselves, to grow at their own pace, to connect in ways that resonate with their lifestyle, and to experience maximum safety and stability, within the boundaries of the life-changing message of the gospel. "Finding the balance between all these competing tensions is the art in ministry. Especially in our culture, which values religion but not Christianity, and which treasures personal growth but believes that can happen without a serious commitment to spiritual formation."

Paul entered the pastorate because he wanted to teach people about Jesus and the Christian way of life. His dominant frustration has been in trying to lead the church forward. "I am a strong believer in leadership by consensus.

People don't want a pastor who is a dictator; they want one who is a shepherd, a loving overseer who provides guidance through biblical teaching and reinforcement through positive encouragement.

"Yes, the church needs to embrace some types of changes, but those changes must be embraced by the people. A pastor cannot jam changes down the throats of the people and expect them to like it or expect to get positive results. So, my ministry has been to stir a level of sensitivity to new perspectives, and then to facilitate discussions and planning sessions that generate agreement on how to proceed.

"At least, in seminary that's what they taught us leadership was all about; the new material coming out these days paints a very different picture. Frankly, leading my church has been the single least rewarding task as pastor. I don't see myself as a visionary, but as a shepherd, so focusing people on a long-range view of where we are going is very hard for me. Half the time I'm not sure myself!

"I like to take things slowly, one day at a time, and reflect rather than react. I've seen so many churches get themselves in a bind because they moved too quickly, or because they cut loose from their history and foundation. I think my style is reasonable, but the results sometimes betray that view.

"The whole emphasis on team leadership that is in vogue these days is a comfortable fit for me, at least theoretically. But when you get twelve elders in the room to discuss an issue, you wind up with twelve different notions of how to move ahead. Everyone has their own agenda, their own methods, and nobody is willing to give an inch. If I try to firmly direct the process, to move things along, I'm accused of being a control freak. If I get the people more intimately involved and allow them greater authority and decision-making power, I'm criticized as weak and visionless. So often it seems like a no-win situation for me.

"I love the teaching aspect of my job, and I can get by when it comes to planning, but resolving the disputes, focusing people's attention, mobilizing people, and generating the resources to enable change, all of that is not my strong suit."

In the end, Paul has resolved that the benefit he uniquely brings to the church is his knowledge of the Bible and his ability to help people understand its timeless truths. He has tried to bridge the past and future through his teaching by helping people understand the basis of the Bible, the historic creeds of the church, the genesis of the church's traditions, and the role of God's people in influencing the world. He has encouraged them to reach out by pointing out the unique functions people of faith can play in a world of seekers, doubters, and complacent observers. He initiates discussions about strategic decisions: whether to focus on in-reach or outreach, whether to grow the church through events or advertising or relationships, and so forth. Even so, he remains frustrated by the tensions that define his daily efforts.

WHEN CHURCH GOALS
CONFLICT WITH PASTORAL GIFTS

Paul's sense of frustration is shared by many of his colleagues. The vast majority of those who go into full-time ministry do so because they feel they have a gift for teaching. Unfortunately, the dreams of these young ministers are dashed once they graduate; they soon discover that pastors must fill leadership roles for which they were not trained, and which they often do not feel capable of handling.

In reviewing the notes from a recent elders' meeting at his church, some of the constraints under which Paul operates become readily apparent. A number of issues had been addressed that appeared to define Paul's assignment:

- attract and keep more visitors;
- raise more money so the church can fund the ministry agenda approved by the elders;
- raise the community's awareness of the church; and
- expand the roster of ministries and programs under the church's umbrella.

To his board, these criteria are the measures of success. As a student and teacher of the Bible, those measures irritate Paul because they have so much to do with leadership and management, and so little to do with whether or not people know Christ, follow Him, and make Him known to others.

Paul is not alone in his dilemma. Caught between their calling and the pressures placed upon them by denominational officers or lay leadership to demonstrate immediate, substantial progress, many ministers vacate their post before they ever have a chance to succeed.

Studies show that senior pastors typically experience their major impact during the fifth through fourteenth years of tenure. However, the average tenure of a senior pastor in American churches has dropped to just *four years.* In other words, many pastors must resign themselves to a life of frustration because they are changing positions before they are able to see the fruit of the early years of their administration.

Other pastors like the *idea* of being leaders, but are not gifted to fulfill that role. Consequently, some pastors establish pseudo-leadership patterns that are not conducive to true Christian leadership. Examples of these kinds of leaders include:

The Drill Sergeant. Drill Sergeants love to be in charge, to have control. They take great pleasure in ordering people around. They demand people's compliance through sheer aggression. These individuals rule through fear, guilt, pressure, and position, rather than devotion to God, His vision, and His people.

However, giving orders does not make a person a leader any more than flying in an airplane makes a person a bird. The qualities exhibited by the Drill Sergeant are a stark departure from those of a true Christian leader. In the Church, a leader is a servant. True leaders recognize their own limitations and see their leadership as a calling, not a means of satisfying deep-seated emotional needs. True leaders feel compelled to lead—they can't stand being in the midst of non-leaders who attempt to lead—but they do not have to force themselves upon a group of people.

The Robot. When Robots are placed in leadership positions, they operate as if on automatic pilot. They carry out rote tasks, stifle creativity, and set survival as the standard of success. Conflicts are covered up, new ideas tabled, and manners and symbols esteemed above content and impact. The Robot equates predictability with security. Vision is perceived a nuisance; passion is depreciated.

True Christian leaders recognize that ministry is about taking risks, but have the intelligence to manage those risks and the faith to trust God in situations when risks seem warranted. A ministry without a passion for God and His vision is simply an exercise in futility under the banner of religion. No true leader would allow passion for ministry to be extinguished.

The Monarch. Monarchs are individuals who have been elevated to a position of leadership as a career reward for having played by the rules, not as a ministry calling. These individuals assume that others will follow by virtue of the Monarch's status and reputation, regardless of his or her abilities, experiences, preparation, or gifts. Legalism is a prominent character trait of the Monarch; vision plays a very minor role in the administration of such leaders.

This leadership type bears no resemblance to the true Christian leader, either. Leadership is not a prize to be won; those who have been called by God to lead are often not those who have "paid the dues," in the normal manner of speaking. Often they do not even seek the positions of leadership that are thrust upon them due to the undeniable power of their leadership gift.

In times of rapid or significant change—and ours is a time of both—success is most likely to be achieved when a strong leader continually reinforces a genuine and powerful vision for the future. Organizations that run aground during times of instability invariably lack vision or strong leaders—or both.

Without strong leadership, chaos and deterioration prevail. The absence of vision during times of change results in a focus on the past, which in turn generates unrealistic plans and unhealthy conflict. Unable to instigate real progress, the group begins to dissipate.

The future of the Church largely depends upon the emergence of leaders— not necessarily seminary graduates, pastors, or professional clergy, but individuals called by God to lead—who will commit their lives to the Church and cast God's vision for ministry without flinching. These anointed ones will motivate people to get involved, and lead the way in amassing the resources necessary to complete the required tasks. They will mobilize a team of leaders and other gifted specialists, incite them to create innovative solutions to emerging obstacles, push them to evaluate their efforts and outcomes with honesty, and encourage them to keep taking rational risks in their relentless pursuit of God's vision.[1]

AREN'T ALL PASTORS CALLED TO BE LEADERS?

Perhaps you are perplexed by this discussion about the need for leaders within the Church. We have over one-half million seminary graduates in America, most of whom are serving the body of believers in a full-time ministry capacity. Could it be possible that the American church is in need of more leaders?

Most American churches have a senior pastor who provides what could be considered the primary leadership for that congregation. Some are outstanding teachers, others are gifted administrators, still others have well-developed "people skills" that enable them to minister in sensitive situations.

HOW CHRISTIAN LEADERS AND CHRISTIAN TEACHERS DIFFER

How leaders operate	*How teachers operate*
Influence via vision and character	Influence via ideas and words
Provide direction and motivation	Provide intellectual challenge
Seek corporate transformation	Seek individual growth
Love to strategize	Love to study
Need a core of committed zealots	Need a teachable audience
Know when to make unpopular decisions	Teach the truth, even when unpopular
Motivate people to action	Motivate people to think
Resolve conflict	Stir up conflict

However, not all these pastors have the gift of leadership. When we ask pastors to identify their greatest frustrations in the pastorate, leadership activities top the list. Our research among senior pastors of Protestant churches has revealed the following:

- Less than one out of every ten senior pastors can articulate what he believes is God's vision for the church he is leading.

- Only 5 percent of senior pastors say they have the gift of leadership. Most pastors thought they were neither called to nor divinely equipped for that post.

- A time-management study we conducted among pastors showed that the typical pastor works long hours (more than sixty hours per week), but devotes less than ten hours per week to leadership activities. Naturally, leading a complex organization such as a church demands substantial amounts of focused time. Part of the reason they devote so few hours to leadership endeavors is because of the extensive and often unreasonable expectations of what a pastor can accomplish.

When pastors are asked what they enjoy most about their job, teaching and preaching top the list. It's little wonder: Most of them believe they have the spiritual gift of teaching or preaching, and most of them spent a number of years in seminary honing their abilities of exegeting the Bible and communicating its truths.

Our research confirms that, like Paul Corrales, most pastors are teachers. Teaching and leading are related but distinct. Some unique individuals have been called and gifted by God to be both a teacher and a leader, but our studies indicate that those individuals are the exception to the rule. Consequently, most pastors put as little time into leadership activities as they feel they must in order to get by. *Most senior pastors serving churches today are not truly leaders, although they hold a position of leadership.*

It is nothing short of tragic that the Church expects pastors—individuals who love God and are devoted to serving Him—to satisfy two unique roles that require different abilities, gifts, and preparation. This unreasonable expectation sets up the congregation for frustration and the pastor for failure. The problem is magnified by our tendency to hold up large churches with unusually gifted leaders as the norm and expect all pastors to live up to the levels reached by those special leaders.

So what's the solution? Certainly not to drum teachers out of full-time ministry simply because they are not leaders. God has called all of us to certain duties and gifted us in specific ways for the building up of the Church. To banish teachers and preachers would be to commit the same sin against them as we currently commit against leaders who are prevented from exercising their gift.

HOW LEADERS AND MANAGERS DIFFER

How leaders operate	_How managers operate_
Conceptualize outcomes by working from the future back to the present	Conceptualize plans by working from the present to the future
Focus on the long-term	Focus on the short-term
Embrace a macro perspective	Embrace a micro perspective
Favor innovative thinking	Favor routine thinking
Balance idealism and realism	Emphasize pragmaticism over idealism
Revolutionary flair	Protector of the status quo
Emphasis on what and why	Emphasis on how and when
Clarifies the vision	Implements the vision
Inspiring and motivating	Controlling and directing
Excited by change	Threatened by change
Identifies opportunities	Identifies obstacles
Takes risks	Avoids risks
Pursues acquisition of resources	Action limited by available resources
Person-centered, idea-centered	Systems-centered, plan-centered

The solution is to utilize the special and necessary gift teachers and preachers bring to the Church, while releasing them from the burdens of leading people. In other words, we ought to create teams of capable individuals who have complementary gifts and abilities so that the Church can move forward strategically and efficiently. We will explore this further in Chapter 8.

A PROFILE OF PROTESTANT PASTORS, 1997
BASE: 601 PASTORS

Pastor's x	_1997_
Male	95%
Average age (in years)	48
Married	95%
College graduate	88%
Spiritual gifts:	
—preaching/teaching	69%
—pastoring	15%
—administration	15%
—exhortation, encouragement	11%
—evangelism	6%
—leadership	5%
Years in full-time ministry	17
Years at current church	5
Annual compensation package ($000)	36.4

Source: Barna Research Group, Ltd., Oxnard, CA; PastorPoll™; 1997.

IS THERE AN ALTERNATIVE?

By Sunday night, Paul is exhausted. He works sixty to sixty-five hours a week, juggling a host of responsibilities in the church and trying to keep his family life under control when he gets away from the church. His wife and two ado-lescent children are understanding and supportive, but he realizes that they get only the leftovers of his mind and energy.

He once attended a conference on the importance of balancing personal and pastoral life, but it wasn't much help or consolation. "I'd sit there for two or three days, taking notes, thinking about the information and principles, and then I'd realize I was only being made to feel worse because I couldn't attain the standards these speakers were setting for me.

"I think the hard truth is that you marry your ministry. For centuries the Catholic Church has maintained that a priest or pastor is married to God and his life must reflect that priority. It's not a politically correct perspective, but there's probably more truth to it than we give it credit for."

Paul worries about the future of the Church. He sees the growing gap between the paths being pursued by the population and that offered by churches. But he constantly reminds himself that "we are to be in the world, not of it. Jesus told His disciples that His church will prevail, and you either believe that the Lord knew what He was talking about or you don't. If you do, then you also have to believe that much of what we are experiencing today is beyond our comprehension, maybe even beyond our control, and that being the Church is as much a matter of faith as believing in Christ is a matter of faith.

"Everyday I see God do miracles—little miracles, but miracles neverthe-less—and it helps me to maintain a proper perspective. In the end, Christ wins and so do we, if we believe. We can't get too bent out of shape over the daily pressures and struggles that would steal away the joy of knowing that when it's all over, we were on the winning team. That's the hope that I cling to for myself, my family, my church, and our world."

[F O U R]
ONE SIZE DOES NOT FIT ALL

WHEN PAUL WILCOX ASSUMED the pastorate at King of Kings Lutheran, he knew that his new church had been going nowhere fast, for more than a decade. And he was well aware of the price he would pay for instituting the types of changes he had described when the search committee interviewed him, and again when the elder board met with him before voting on his candidacy.

King of Kings was a classic church in denial—one that knew it had to implement some significant changes, but one that was digging in to fight those necessary transitions every step of the way. "It was one of those situations where I knew what had to be done and that it wasn't going to be easy," recalled Pastor Wilcox. "But the situation was quite clear. We could deny our predicament, keep telling ourselves it'd all work out if we just keep on going the same way, and eventually get beyond the point of being a salvageable ministry. Or, we could face the music, recognize the need to make some tough decisions and change direction, and maybe become a healthy church once again."

Unlike most churches, King of Kings was able to become a healthy church after nearly a decade of hard choices, prayer, heavy investment, and managed risks. Ask Pastor Wilcox how he managed to lead a recalcitrant church to stability and he does not hesitate. "My primary challenge was to make sure that we made strategic choices. I did everything I could to make sure that we all realized that the best course of action for us—for King of Kings, right here, downtown—might be totally different from what worked for other churches. The programs that work well at Willow or Wooddale or Saddleback are great, but they might not be appropriate for us. We had to examine the principles and strategies that enabled those programs to work in those places and then translate those principles to our own community. I was blessed to have a group of laity who recognized that our path to victory required us to understand our circumstances and opportunities, and to act in a strategic way."

Jim Stockton was the founding pastor of a rapidly growing midsize church in the Midwest. He echoed the same emphasis upon understanding the context and adapting the church to the changing ministry context. "When I started here nine years ago we followed a ministry growth plan I had developed after studying the city for about eighteen months. But if we were to start the church today that same plan would fail—things have changed that much. In fact, we have scrapped that original plan—and the one we created after that—because of all the new changes that have redefined this area. We have an entire group of people from the congregation whose primary gift of service to this church is sensitizing us to emerging trends that will affect our ministry. Last year's plan was great for last year. But what we need is this year's plan for next year—and to constantly update that thinking. It's like they say: You snooze, you lose."

Strategic change is the lifeblood of longevity and influence in today's marketplace. In fact, remaining well informed and poised to act quickly has never been so important.

As stated earlier, cultural analysts presently estimate that our culture essentially reinvents itself every three to five years. In other words, the core attributes of our society—language, customs, dress styles, dominant leisure pursuits, relational emphases, values, and the like—are being substantially reshaped and reconfigured every few years. Although we are accustomed to thinking of our society as stable and consistent, many of the central defining elements of our culture are undergoing constant redefinition. The failure to deal with those changes is the fastest and surest route to extinction.

It is not necessary that organizations, causes, or movements totally make themselves over two or three times per decade. But entities that wish to have influence within our culture must demonstrate a willingness and ability to adapt to the changing environment. In this sense, Darwin's notion of "survival of the fittest" aptly describes what happens in organizations and groups striving to achieve and maintain significance in contemporary society.

ENABLING MEANINGFUL CHANGE

Coping with rapid, fundamental, continual change is perhaps more difficult for the Church than for almost any other group. When changes occur that affect a for-profit business, those in charge must determine how those changes impact its bottom line, its core operating values, its existing relationships, and its production procedures and capacity.

When Christ's representatives address changes in their environment, the choices they make and the manner in which they respond to new opportunities, limitations, and conditions are even more significant. In addition to considering how their decisions will affect the physical and temporal needs of people, the Church must also consider the eternal spiritual consequences. Thus, one of the keys to serving Christ effectively is modeling for the world how to appropriately anticipate and respond to change in our culture. Our response should reflect the practical and appropriate application of the timeless truths and principles of the Bible.

Christians and churches make two types of blunders when it comes to handling change:

They refuse to change when change is called for. Or, if they do not refuse altogether, they delay making the necessary changes until it is too late.

One of the most important lessons the American church must absorb is that patience may be harmful to the Church's health. People need spiritual solutions now! We live in the age of impatience. People want the results they desire, and they demand those outcomes be delivered faster than ever before.

Consider the progression of experience in the secular communications industry. When an important meeting is called, people used to board trains or buses to get to the meeting place; then airplanes; now companies are turning to videoconferencing. Federal Express forever changed the way we do business by introducing overnight delivery service. But that wasn't fast enough. Facsimile machines made the delivery of important documents virtually immediate. But this was still not fast enough. Today, E-mail is threatening to make fax machines dinosaurs.

Companies used to take up to seven years to develop a new product; that time frame has been consistently reduced. Now, the average new product must be developed in sixteen months or less or it is deemed a failure before it is even released!

Americans will choose speed over depth every time. Because our time is limited and there are so many experiences we'd like to have, speed is attractive. We'll take the quick fix over the laborious renovation. We prefer immediate profits to building a strong financial base for the future. Loyalty is a thing of the past; we often relinquish long-term relationships in favor of new relationships that promise more immediate, higher quality results.

The Church does not have the luxury of time to ponder all the ins and outs of how to best reconstitute itself. People are very busy. Most Americans have very tenuous ties to the Church. While the window of opportunity is open, the Church must jump through it or lose a precious chance to be agents of life transformation to those who still value and trust the input the Church has to offer.

The second type of mistake many churches make is "change for the sake of change," resulting in indefensible or inappropriate decisions. The simple truth is that there is no single product that will meet everyone's needs all the time. However, people expect high quality and a customized, relevant solution to their needs. There is little room for error. If those that a church is seeking to reach do not feel that the services and programs offered were created for them, they will leave without a second thought.

The Church of the future must be a community of faith that facilitates highly personalized and focused ministry. Knowing why, when, and how to change are important insights that must direct our efforts to contextualize our lives and ministries without compromising the fundamental truths and principles that define our faith.

THE CHURCH MUST PLAN FOR SUCCESS

If we are to experience the second coming of the Church, we must learn from past failures in order to plan strategically for the future.

One of these lessons is that we must have a clear operational definition of success. The old adage says, "If you don't know where you're going, any road will take you there." That's been a dilemma of the American church. We traverse routes that take us places that don't seem right, but we really don't know if our destinations are appropriate or not because we never defined what we were striving to achieve.

Which brings us to a second important lesson: We must be able to measure that success. Self-assessment is an indispensable part of determining the health of a ministry. This includes both establishing individual accountability in the lives of believers as well as defining corporate ministry success in ways that can be measured and tracked.

WHAT CONSTITUTES MINISTRY SUCCESS?

Almost every church I have worked with or studied performs some level of self-evaluation. Most commonly, churches seek to determine if they are "growing" or "successful."

In most cases, when I have asked church leaders to define ministry success, they invariably produce a mission statement or some other document that specifies the outcomes that constitute success. Worship, evangelism, giving, prayer, discipleship, and social service are among the items usually listed as the indicators of significant ministry. The factors listed are usually laudable and biblically defensible.

However, in most cases the values contained in these mission statements do not surface to any great degree in the life of the church itself. In spite of what the leaders claim the criteria for evaluation are, I have found that there are usually five primary criteria used to evaluate the aggregate health of the ministry. These outcomes are as follows:

Congregational size. It would appear that the Sunday morning head count is considered to be the best measure of a church's vitality. The assumption seems to be that the more people who attend the church, the more successful is the church. Many pastors dream of heading up a megachurch; many parishioners buy into that dream.

Church facility. Many pastors are convinced that a church must possess more than a mere building; it needs a campus. For many churches, it is no longer sufficient to have a place in which people worship God; now the church must own the space. The perception is that a truly successful church develops an entire campus to sustain an ever-broadening ministry.

Scope of ministry. Most churches contend that they must have something for everyone. We have come to believe that every church must take care of every need of every person who might ever have any interaction with the organization. Consequently, we initiate and try to maintain as broad an agenda of ministries and programs as possible.

Budget size. The dominant view these days is that a large budget is a sign of God's blessing on the ministry. Money facilitates ministry activity, so naturally churches evaluate their funding trends. A growing budget is seen as evidence of congregational commitment, ownership of the mission, and sacrificial living.

Pastoral credibility. A pastor's public persona must be above reproach. Because the pastor is the most visible representative of the congregation, and is supposed to set an example for the church, the lay leaders evaluate the level of public integrity demonstrated by the pastor. However, there is typically little assessment beyond the pastor's public image and actions.

PRESERVATION, OR TRUE GROWTH?

Unfortunately, these factors are barely an adequate starting point for truly evaluating the quality of a church's ministry and character. They do not do justice to the magnificent mandate given to us by our Lord, and they trivialize the meaning of serious Christianity and impair the prospects of spiritual rebirth and revitalization.

We will explore more fully in Chapter 7 the principles contained in Scripture to establish the "unsinkable" true Church. But first, let's consider the reason church leaders are redefining the standards for effective church ministry. In essence, over the course of time, the drive for self-preservation overwhelms the desire for true growth.

It might be useful to realize that every organization goes through stages of growth. The most widely accepted perspective on corporate life maintains that there are four major periods or cycles. These cycles are also recognizable within Christian ministries.

1. *The infancy or "birthing" phase.* During the initial period of development, the relationships that comprise the community of faith, the vision that powers the ministry, and the values that define its character are formed. It is usually loosely structured but maintains a high energy level among its members. The focus of the group is directed largely to the future.

2. *The development or "growth" phase.* This period occurs after the first five to ten years of ministry. It is during this time that the ministry develops in size and scope. The emphasis during this period is upon expansion in people, programs, resources, and facilities that will achieve critical mass sufficient to fulfill that ministry's objectives.

3. *The mature phase.* At this stage of development, a ministry runs smoothly because the necessary systems have been developed and refined. The primary focus is on smooth operation of the ministry: Continuity and consistency assume top priority. While the environment continues to change, fewer risks are taken and changes occur more slowly. The group begins to focus more and more on its history rather than its future.

4. *The declining phase.* This is every ministry's "final frontier." During this phase, the church has clearly lost its energy because it has fulfilled its purpose or has become too complacent in its past achievements or present comfort. As it begins to wind down, the organization gradually loses people, resources, and influence. The primary goal changes from growth to mere survival.[1]

As they progress through each life cycle and become increasingly institutionalized, many churches (and Christians, for that matter) become obsessed with self-preservation. Every year millions and millions of dollars and thousands upon thousands of hours are poured into maintaining dead churches. But where in Scripture does it say that a congregation, as an organization, must endure forever?

One of the fundamental lessons drawn from organizational research is that unless intentional self-renewal is built into the developmental process, every organization will die. Unless an organization purposefully alters the natural progression, it is only a matter of time before all four phases have been experienced.

Escaping death after entering the decline phase is very difficult—and the longer it stays mired in decline, the less likely renewal becomes. The only suitable course of action is for the church to embark on an intentional campaign designed to introduce radical reinvigoration (new vision from God, or the integration of a new core congregation).

The only thing that Jesus came to preserve was people's souls—not cultures, religious institutions, families, religious traditions, or the like. Our emphasis must be similar as we prepare for the future Church.

CULTURAL AND DEMOGRAPHIC
TRENDS IN AMERICAN SOCIETY

[FIVE]
THE NEW CULTURAL REALITIES

AMERICA IS A COMPLEX SOCIETY. While our population is fragmented on many levels—ethnically, regionally, economically, and socially—the resulting diversity has greatly benefited us. One of the primary benefits is a richness of experiences, perspectives, goals, and energy that is absent in static, homogeneous societies.

On the other hand, the challenges associated with population growth and diversity have exacted a stiff price on our culture. The proximity of differing and often conflicting values and belief systems contributes to the moral relativity that plagues our nation. And the process of assimilating people into an orderly and progressive cultural mix is an extraordinarily difficult challenge.

In our nation, the disparities between rich and poor, educated and uneducated, married and single, conservatives and liberals, urban, suburban and rural, American-born and foreign-born, Christian and non-Christian, and child-bearing and childless have become more pronounced and divisive than ever. Yet, the failure to orchestrate a comfortable blend of relationships, behaviors, and opportunities among these groups has resulted in a certain amount of cultural dissipation. Hostility, mistrust, chaos, anomie, apathy, and lack of productivity are among the chief outcomes when such conflicts cannot be strategically resolved.

While most churches continue to pursue a one-size-fits-all ministry strategy, the culture in which we live is too diverse and values customization too highly to expect that we can fulfill every need by implementing a single set of programs, events, language, and symbols. To be effective, we must learn to target our efforts and to contextualize what we have to offer to others so that they see our offering as relevant, beneficial, and accessible.[1]

[51]

UNDERSTANDING AND EMBRACING
CULTURAL DIVERSITY

To remain relevant and influential, we must be current in our understanding of cultural changes and their implications. The changes that influence our lives and ministry fall within these key domains: *demographics, attitudes and values, lifestyles and behaviors, and spirituality.*

Within each of those categories of change, we must consider not only the nature of the changes taking place, but also the underlying perspectives and needs that drive those changes as well as the cultural and ministry implications of each change.[2] We have already explored many of the current spiritual trends in America today. Let's consider the trends related to the other categories of cultural design.

Understanding demographic trends can permit a church to increase its responsiveness to the emerging needs and expectations of the community it seeks to serve. By understanding changes in basic characteristics that impact how we view and experience reality—attributes such as age, education, ethnicity, and income—we raise our probability of developing ministry solutions to the real needs of the people.

DEMOGRAPHIC TRENDS

Ethnicity

America's population continues to grow at a significant pace, netting roughly three million people per year (four million births plus one million immigrants less two million deaths). However, the population grows for different reasons today than in the past.

Twenty years ago, the vast majority of American families were white, and most babies were born to families headed by white married couples. This is no longer the case. Today, Caucasians in the United States are at zero population growth: They are bearing enough children to "replace" those who die but not enough to expand the size of the Caucasian population.

Our minority populations, however, are growing.[3] This is attributable to two factors: increased immigration and the fact that minority populations have a greater number of children per family.

Based on current projections, during the 1990s the African American segment will have grown by 15 percent, the Hispanic population will have increased by about 39 percent, and the Asian community will have jumped by about 40 percent. This is a process of change that is expected to continue for the long-term. The Census Bureau informs us that while three out of four Americans are presently Caucasian, by 2050 only half of the nation will be Caucasian. For this reason, multiculturalism will be increasingly significant in our language, customs, values, relationships, and processes.

How do these realities impact Christian ministry? The Church cannot afford to ignore the realities of cultural diversity. The outreach methods and procedures that were effective in the past are no longer relevant to a population that is so racially and ethnically diversified. The values and needs of each group are radically different; worship, evangelism, Christian education, stewardship, and discipleship goals must be tailored to the needs of each group.

However, before the Church can begin to adapt its programs to the needs of the various ethnic groups represented within the community, we must take a hard look at ourselves. While younger segments of the population have grown accustomed to living in an ethnically diverse society, older generations—Seniors, Builders, and Boomers—have traditionally been resistant to these changes. We cannot expect to influence our community for good until we repent of racist attitudes, inaccurate assumptions, and unrealistic expectations related to racial diversity.

Our nation continues to be troubled by racial and ethnic hostilities: whites versus blacks, blacks versus Hispanics, blacks versus Asians, whites versus Hispanics. Though the need for racial and ethnic reconciliation has been widely discussed, and numerous efforts have been made in that regard, the population remains resistant to solutions.

How can the Church help? We must start with ourselves. Until Sunday morning ceases to be the most racially segregated time of the week, the Church will never be a major agent of influence in racial matters. When it comes to racial harmony, those who are paying attention recognize the gap between what we preach and what we do.

Wealth

The American economy is a study in extremes. On the one hand, we have more wealthy people than any other nation of the world. On the other hand, we have millions of people living in dire poverty.

The cumulative, personal net worth of Americans continues to grow. It is currently estimated that our net worth exceeds $22 trillion. In fact, we now have more than three million households in the United States considered "wealthy"—having a net worth in excess of $1 million.[4]

Most of this is "new money"—wealth generated by those who currently possess it. Eighty percent of the millionaires in America did not come from affluent families. A variety of studies have indicated that the wealthiest Americans possess a disproportionate amount of the nation's wealth.

There is a down side to this. Government statistics suggest that we have more than thirty million people living in poverty and the true figure is probably considerably higher if we use a measure of poverty more realistic than that used by the federal government. No matter how you evaluate poverty, though, many economists agree that among the developed nations of the world, America's wealth is distributed most unequally.[5]

The government-sponsored safety net for the poor is gradually being removed, leaving the poor to fend for themselves. Amazingly, growing numbers of Americans are exhibiting a hardened heart toward the plight of the less fortunate. Research indicates that even Christian churches are less frequently involved in compassion ministries and are allocating less money than they used to toward addressing the needs of the poor in their own communities.

Sadly, America is not the land of opportunity it once was. As America transitions into a service-based economy, the job market will reflect a growing number of minimum wage and low-paying jobs, reducing the opportunities for those on the outside to enter into the land of plenty. Climbing costs for education, real estate, and the cost of living overall will contribute to the escalation of personal debt levels, threatening the economic security of many who presently live on or near the financial edge.

This is especially bad news for those in the Buster generation, who tend to switch careers numerous times during their working years (in search of new experiences and challenges, rather than economic ascendancy). This could limit their earnings potential.

The Church must consider carefully how it will respond to this situation. As the government seeks to unload the responsibility of caring for the poor upon churches and other nonprofit organizations, new economic tensions will arise. Given the declining interest in compassion ministries, the costly church-related construction projects initiated each year (more than $2 billion initiated by churches annually), and the changing donation patterns and habits of Americans, it seems likely that growing numbers of economically disadvantaged people will continue to struggle.

Education

The educational system in America is in shambles. Last year more than a million teenagers received their high school diploma even though they couldn't read it!

Kids graduating from high school are monumentally ill-prepared to handle the world. Fiscal realities have forced schools to cut back to the barest basics. Consequently, kids are less likely to learn necessary skills; many extra-curricular and nonacademic programs that have traditionally rounded out a student's skill base and life perspectives have been eliminated.

Sadly, a basic shift in educational philosophy has left our youth deprived of training in areas that represent "soft skills." Schools have increased their emphasis upon "hard skills" such as mathematics and language skills, partially because those are the factors on which students are tested and thus schools can be evaluated. "Soft skills," which refers to abilities affecting interpersonal behavior, get neglected because they are less measurable and deemed to be less valid as educational foci. As a result, students are less comfortable and less well-prepared to engage in relationship building, listening, conflict resolution, negotiating, team building, and creative problem solving.

Other fiscal realities hit closer to home: Career pressures are causing parents from dual-income families to have less and less involvement in the education of their own children. Those young people who go to college are now taking an average of five and one-half years to finish their degree—if they complete their studies at all—due to the typical costs and other limitations.

As we have already touched upon in Chapter 3, technology plays an increasingly major role in the education of our children, through new hardware and software applications that remove the human touch, and which have resulted in an entirely new style of thinking among our children.

How can Christians respond? The inadequacies of the educational system have already prompted some reaction within the Christian community. One response has been the home schooling movement. This trend has seen significant growth in recent years, predominantly among Christian families who are concerned about the quality of the values, relationships, and skills taught to their children.

Although home schooling will remain an alternative relatively few families can or will embrace—currently, less than one million of our forty million households with school-age children are involved in home schooling—it reflects a conscious reaction to the dominant methods and outcomes of our educational system. And yet, while this educational trend is commendable, the Church must dig deeper when considering how we must respond to the cultural realities that this dearth of education has and will continue to produce. As literacy levels decline and visual communication ascends in significance, we must rethink our methods of communication.

The fact that half of today's adults cannot read or write at an eighth-grade level has grave consequences for all levels of church ministry. People's levels of confidence in traditional forms of communication (such as the printed word) and in the integrity of popular communication media (such as television and radio) have declined precipitously. (Question to consider: Does it make sense to spend so much money broadcasting your Sunday morning worship service?)

Attention spans are getting shorter all the time; among teenagers, the average is six to eight minutes. An increasing degree of learning is taking place through informal observation, rather than through listening to lectures or reading reasoned arguments. If we are going to effectively reach the world around us for Christ, now more than ever people will be attracted by what we *do* rather than what we *say*.

Essential principles of postmodern communication. One of the challenges the new Church must face is how to communicate effectively with the intended audience. This challenge is relevant to ministries whether they are old-school congregational churches, emerging church forms, or parachurch entities.

Increasingly, we are working in a postmodern environment, in which beliefs, values, lifestyles, and even styles of learning have changed dramatically from those that were commonplace thirty years ago. As teachers of God's Word, we must never compromise the core of our message; however, the communication media, styles, and strategies used to convey God's message to His people must change over the course of time because culture and context are constantly changing.

Effective communication is an art, but it is founded upon some core principles.

- Effective communicators understand *how an audience absorbs information.*

- Effective communicators understand *what an audience will pay attention to.*

- Effective communicators convey *a clear and meaningful message to the audience.*

- Effective communicators *seek and evaluate feedback* so that subsequent communications will continue to hit the mark and have the desired influence.

At present the Church is intensely geared to pastors and other seminary-trained staff disseminating accurate and appropriate theological knowledge; in the future, an increasing proportion of Bible teaching and theological education will be conducted by laypeople. But conveying Bible truths and related information in the same ways we have always done— ways most churches seem committed to continuing—will further hamper our potential to penetrate a changing society with God's timeless and priceless truths.

The content and delivery style of much of the current teaching and preaching in churches is designed for an older audience. That is largely because many teachers and preachers have yet to accept a critical reality: Churches are now serving a new majority. Although people over the age of fifty are more likely to attend church services, Busters and Boomers outnumber their elders by a three-to-two margin in church attendance. In other words, about 60 percent of the adults exposed to sermons in Christian churches on any given weekend are less than fifty years old. In fact, with each passing day, those over fifty dwindle in number, effectively elevating the dominance of the younger audience.

Here's why this is so significant. We have learned that the under-fifty crowd receives and interprets information differently from their older counterparts.

- *Younger adults are accustomed to receiving information at a faster rate than older adults.* Pacing has become a crucial element in determining whether or not the typical listener sticks with an entire sermon.

- *Time is treasured.* Long before they are concluded sermons tend to lose younger listeners. Among the younger Busters, the tendency is to tune out after six to eight minutes—unless there is some type of transition that renews their interest.

- *Words are important.* The language a communicator uses will largely determine the receptivity of the audience. Language that is theological, judgmental, or incessantly paternalistic creates problems for many younger listeners.

- *Attitude is everything.* Audiences who perceive speakers as arrogant or insensitive won't give them the benefit of the doubt.

- *The medium used to transmit information impacts the perceived credibility of that information.* Information conveyed through the use of technology often has a higher degree of believability than does information coming directly out of a speaker's mouth.

If we are going to be effective, credible witnesses to the younger generations, we cannot afford to lose sight of these educational and communication-oriented principles.

TRENDS IN VALUES AND ATTITUDES

Philosophy of Life

Most Americans claim they have a carefully conceived philosophy of life. The vast majority of those individuals also claim to be Christian and that their worldview is centered on biblical values. Our research, however, reaches a different conclusion.

First, most adults live for the moment and have nothing more than a loose set of ideals and principles to which they cling. These ideals often conflict with one another (for example, love your neighbor; always look out for your own best interests) and are frequently abandoned during times of stress, crisis, opportunity, or confusion.

Second, the basis of people's philosophy, even in its unsophisticated state, is not Christianity as much as existentialism. This is often referred to as a postmodernist line of reasoning. Its essentials are as follows:

- *There is no grand purpose to life.* The reason for living is to achieve comfortable survival. Success is defined as the absence of pain and sacrifice, and the experience of happiness.

- *There is no value to focusing on or preparing for the future.* Every person must live in the moment and for the moment.

- *There are no absolutes.* All spiritual and moral principles are relative to the situation and the individual.

- *There is no omnipotent, all-knowing deity that guides reality.* We must lean on our own vision, competencies, power, and perceptions to make the most of life.

Most Americans possess an entitlement mentality: We believe we deserve every possible good and positive outcome, without having to earn those outcomes. You can imagine the challenges inherent in convincing people that their foundational perspectives are fundamentally wrong. Most Americans do not recognize the underlying existentialist or postmodernist undertones to their belief system; they truly believe they are practicing Christian beliefs, values, and principles.

Those who use empirical evidence to identify the discrepancies between postmodern views and behaviors and those defined in Scripture are typically dismissed as fundamentalist fanatics or judgmental religious zealots. Effectively penetrating the defenses of existentialists requires more relational and creative methods.

Core Values

The "live for the moment" mentality has had a predictable effect on our values system. Buying in to the moral relativity and "political correctness" embraced by our culture, most people no longer deliberately organize their lives around a core value system. Instead, most Americans back into a set of values that remain in force until something better or more appealing comes along. Here are some of the most widely accepted values of Americans today:

- *Time is our single most precious nonrenewable commodity.* Guard your time carefully; use it wisely. Spend money to protect your schedule.

- *Minimize long-term commitments.* Be flexible. Things change too fast to justify permanent commitments, and great opportunities are often unpredictable.

- *Maintain your independence and individuality at all costs.* Possess a healthy skepticism of people, organizations, and philosophies. You are unique and must protect yourself against the vested interests and stacked agendas of those who cannot be trusted to serve your needs and interests.

- *Trust your feelings to guide you.* Relying upon absolute principles places unrealistic limitations on you. Only you know what's right or best for you at any given moment, in those circumstances.

- *Pursue love and acceptance from others with abandon.* Without love and acceptance, you will feel emotionally empty, and that emptiness will undermine every other dimension of your life. Surround yourself with people who appreciate you.

- *Develop competencies only in the aspects of life that are significant to you.*

- *Don't waste your time doing things that do not produce immediate gratification or reward.* That capacity will protect you from unnecessary pain and suffering and will facilitate achieving the quality of life that you desire.

- *Set goals and achieve them.* It is through our achievements that we develop self-esteem, character, reputation, a desirable lifestyle, and a sense of contribution to the world.

- *Have fun.* The highest end of life is to enjoy the opportunities and experiences available to us. Life is too short to devote time and energy to that which is drudgery.

- *Stay in good health.* Eat right, exercise, and take care of your body.

- *Discover and revel in the purpose of your life.* Without this perspective shaping your thoughts and deeds, life is meaningless. Based on your sense of purpose, your decisions will be more consistent and fulfilling.

What does Scripture say about these so-called values? As seductive and pleasing as many of these seem, recognize how they conflict with the values taught in the Bible. However, because so many Americans are desperately seeking to get by from day to day, challenging these underlying values is threatening to many—even when you have a superior set of alternatives to offer.

Americans align themselves with values that give them control. We don't want anyone telling us what, why, how, where, or when to do anything. Any entity that seeks to control how people think, speak, or live automatically raises suspicion. Placing even moderate parameters on people often causes them to rebel against that entity. Millions of Americans have resisted and resented Christianity because they perceive its principles and laws to be limiting rather than freeing.

If the Church is going to effect real change, we must first teach ourselves to recognize these false values, and once again embrace God's principles. It is only then that we will be able to convincingly show people the dangers of embracing values that conflict with God's principles, and to reinforce the difficult but appropriate choices people make on the basis of righteous values. Our relationships, our teachings, and our programs must be wholly consistent with scriptural values. But it is the consistency of our own lives with biblical values that will give us the opportunity to be heard.

Moral Truth

To the average American, truth is relative to one's values and circumstances. Only one out of every four adults—and even fewer teenagers—believe that there is such a thing as absolute moral truth. The Bible is relegated to nothing more than a book of riveting stories and helpful suggestions. Human reason and emotion become the paramount determinants of all that is desirable and appropriate. This condition may be the single most intense threat to the health of the United States and its people.

Consider the social implications. Without an objective standard of right and wrong, laws and regulations become recommendations rather than mandates. Rights are nothing more than sets of competing preferences. There can be no such thing as deception, only differing vantage points. Personal claims to authority and to the exercise of related power are susceptible to unsubstantiated challenges. Without accepted guideline pillars to anchor reality, those who succeed are the ones who argue loudest, most convincingly, and most diligently.

This cultural perspective hardens the hearts and deafens the ears of those who embrace it. Without absolute moral truth, there can be no right and wrong. Without right and wrong, there is no such thing as sin. Without sin, there can be no such thing as judgment and no such thing as condemnation. If there is no condemnation, there is no need for a Savior. This progression renders the death and resurrection of Jesus Christ historically unique—and eternally meaningless.

If those who profess Christ embrace this mind-set, the future looks grim indeed. If we reject the existence of absolute moral truth, such as what the Bible teaches, the Church has nothing to offer our dying culture beyond some nice buildings and programs. Until the Church can persuade people that absolute relativism is not only inherently contradictory but ultimately self-defeating and wrong, all the great biblical teaching we can muster will be negated by a perceptual filter that equates truth with personal preference.

BEHAVIORAL AND LIFESTYLE TRENDS

Longevity

Our flirtation with the latest and greatest reflects an underlying lack of loyalty and commitment to individuals, ideas, and institutions. Significant change can happen overnight; it is difficult to anticipate coming transitions and prepare adequately, to establish credibility and stability, or to build upon past progress.

People change jobs and careers with reckless abandon. It is projected that Baby Busters will change industries—not companies within an industry, mind you, but entire industries—six to twelve times during their working years. (Builders and Seniors typically remained in the same industry for their entire career, while Boomers change industries once or twice.)

This lack of longevity touches the Church as well, further complicating the picture. Building a community of faith is by nature a long-term proposition. Without stability it is difficult to invest in future-oriented outcomes and partnerships. Local churches find themselves always taking one step forward and two steps back because of the constant relearning curve and the loss of expertise and knowledge brought about by continual departures of key players.

If the Church is going to maximize its influence, we must find ways to develop longer-lasting commitments, both to relationships and to ministry plans that cannot be completed in a matter of weeks or months.

Technology

America has been radically redesigned by technology during the nineties. Most households now own at least one computer, and millions use a modem to connect their PC (or TV) to the Internet. The volume of information that is now instantly available to anyone connected to the Net is mind-boggling. In fact, the Internet has changed the locus of power from those who can gather relevant information to those who can now do so instantaneously and then quickly provide the relevant applications of that information.

Cable television continues to provide more and better programming services to people. Radio stations have become more niched. In excess of fifteen thousand different magazine titles are published regularly. The cost of long-distance telephone service has dropped dramatically, while overnight delivery of packages has become commonplace. Satellite conferencing is just starting to become a staple in business circles.

The amount of time we spend involved with mass media (television, radio, newspapers, magazines) and targeted communications media (the Internet, E-mail, faxes) continues to expand. Our recent studies among teenagers show that they devote an average of *seven hours out of their seventeen waking hours each day* to input from the media.

The technological changes that have swept America in the past few years—and the new breakthroughs announced with each passing month—are nothing short of remarkable. But what may be most important are the mental and emotional changes that have permitted such transitions. Consider these five major shifts that have taken place:

- *First, we have compressed the time between the early adoption and mass adoption phases for new electronic and digital products and services.* Americans under the age of forty-five typically accept new equipment and applications at face value; the fear and suspicion that used to accompany the introduction of new products is largely in our past.

- *Second, the integration of technology into every dimension of our lives has raised the expectation of customized products and services.* With the advent of massive databases that enable marketers to track our preferences and respond accordingly, we have grown accustomed to marketing efforts that address our idiosyncrasies. Efforts that smack of generic or mass appeal marketing seem primitive and less appealing.

- *Third, brand names mean less in a pioneering time.* It is the multitude of choices and the freshness of the environment, rather than the predictable availability of time-honored names, traditions, and products, that generate excitement and anticipation.

- *Fourth, we have generally abandoned any sense of filtering incoming communications.* Most people now assume that if it is on TV, the radio, or the Internet, apart from any small warnings regarding dangerous content, all information is created equal and provides value. In an information-driven society, where the distinction between entertainment and information is easily blurred, the notion of "appropriate content" has become anachronistic.

- *Fifth, a major outgrowth of recent (and emerging) technological innovations is decentralization.* People can obtain most of the things they need virtually without ever having to come in contact with another human being. More than one-third of the working population now work from their home instead of a centralized office. Products are marketed to your home via catalogues and on-line services. Relationships are formed via the Internet. A wide array of entertainment events (movies, TV shows, concerts, sports events) is now available almost instantly at the touch of a button.

Where does this leave the Church? These transitions, and others like them, raise new possibilities. Church gatherings represent one of just a handful of remaining opportunities available to people to have regular face-to-face contact with people, other than family, who share their interests and background.

Realize, too, that growing numbers of people now judge the validity and relevance of a church service by the church's use of technology. Their perception, right or wrong, is that if a church is intimately connected to the new digital world then it is more likely to understand their pressures and challenges, and is therefore more likely to offer relevant commentary and solutions.

Lastly, as we will address later in this book, the future of the Church, for millions of Americans, lies on the Internet itself. In just a few years we will see that millions of people will never travel physically to a church, but will instead roam the Internet in search of meaningful spiritual experiences.

Family

Three out of four adults concur that the family unit is weaker today than it was thirty years ago.[6] The litany of changes that have reshaped the family has been well publicized.

- One out of every four marriages has ended in a divorce.

- Two out of three adults say that a successful marriage is one in which both partners have total freedom to do as they choose.

- One-third of all married adults believe that adultery is an acceptable behavior.

- Cohabitation has risen by more than 500 percent in the past two decades (even though people who cohabitate prior to marriage have an 82 percent greater chance of divorce than do couples who marry without having first lived together).

- One out of three children born this year will be born to an unwed mother.

The typical family spends relatively little time in shared emotional experiences, leaving young people with a feeling of emotional abandonment. More than nine out of ten adults have bought into the lie that the most important factor in developing a strong relationship is the quality of the time devoted to the relationship, regardless of the amount of time invested in that bond.

Naturally, much of the thinking that supports such attitudes is a result of moral relativism. But there is another major structural shift, one related to the very definition of family.

In the past, we defined family as people related by birth, adoption, or marriage. Now we define family as all of the people whom we care about very deeply, or who deeply care about us. In fact, our research found that less than half of all adults now believe that if you have a relationship based on birth, adoption, or marriage you are automatically family. These days, you earn your family by virtue of your emotional attachment.

The danger inherent in that definition, of course, is that family then becomes very fluid: Here today, gone tomorrow. This approach to family undermines the potential for trust, loyalty, commitment, forgiveness, sacrifice, and emotional intimacy. It also erodes the stigma associated with behaviors such as adultery, abuse, divorce, and immoral liaisons.

The challenge to the Church is to provide people with more than solid teaching about the importance of family. Americans are willing to accept that; what they say they need, though, are practical helps toward making their family more functional, fulfilling, loving, and growing.

RELIGIOUS AND SPIRITUAL TRENDS[7]

Seven out of ten Americans view themselves as religious. Most of us—86 percent—describe our religious orientation as Christian; a mere 6 percent claim to be atheist or agnostic.

A large percentage (91 percent) say they have a very positive impression of the Christian faith. Every weekend, the number of people attending Christian churches outnumbers those who attend any other type of religious gathering by a ratio of eleven to one.

Nevertheless, Americans are still searching spiritually and willingly admit that their commitment to Christianity is rather lukewarm. Most Americans admit to not yet having found a compelling, defining purpose for their life; millions are steadfastly probing the spiritual domain to facilitate that discovery.

Given our information-rich environment, combined with our exposure to people from other religious backgrounds, more and more Americans are evaluating what other faith groups have to offer in their drive to fulfill their quest for spiritual wisdom and wholeness. In the past such explorations would have been conducted in secret, as if examining faiths other than Christianity were immoral or somehow disrespectful to God.

Things are different today. People brazenly evaluate a variety of faith groups, while maintaining the Christian label. Their unashamed flirtation with hitherto off-limits faith groups is facilitated by core beliefs about the virtue and validity of all faith groups.

Most Americans believe there is no "right" faith; that all of the world's major faiths teach the same lessons; and that all people pray to the same gods, no matter what names they use for those deities. Baby Busters are actually the first generation in American history in which a majority of those who are seeking a religious faith to embrace are starting their spiritual journey with a faith group other than Christianity.[8]

One likely result of this openness to all faiths is that Christianity appears poised to lose "market share" in the coming years. More and more people, enticed by the narcissistic or feel-good focus of other religions, will abandon Jesus Christ in favor of faiths that seem more in tune with their needs.

Diversity and tolerance have clearly edged past the boundaries of political ideology and racial acceptance and invaded the religious realm. For the most part, Americans consider the major faith groups interchangeable: Each faith may have unique language, traditions, icons, and ceremonies, but we view them as unified in their constant push to achieve equivalent outcomes via similar paths of inquiry and activity.

Indeed, given people's underlying assumption that religious faith exists for the personal benefit of the individual, it is only natural for them to assume that defining, organizing, and practicing spirituality in ways that satisfy their personal needs is completely legitimate. One of the chief struggles facing the Christian Church in the days ahead will be to persuade people that the blending of disparate religious beliefs and practices into a customized, impure version of Christianity is illegitimate.

GETTING A GRIP ON REALITY

Do you get a headache—and maybe a heartache—just thinking about how challenging it is to be the Church in such a complex, rapidly changing environment? And the ground we just covered represents only a partial accounting of the numerous issues, changes, and challenges that define American life as we enter the third millennium.

Think of the myriad other critical concerns that we could address to arrive at a truly comprehensive portrait of contemporary reality: relationships, crime, responsibility, gender-based inequities, globalism, business ethics, sexuality, public health, leadership, household finances, and more.

However, even with our relatively cursory evaluation of a limited list of circumstances and related shifts you can see the magnitude of the challenge facing the Church today.

Clearly, to influence the nation with the truths of Christ demands that we be vigilant in tracking the forces of change. Before we can strategically shape or adapt to the challenges before us, we must be aware of and sensitive to those transitions in reality. Only then can we create and implement responses that position us to have influence for God's glory. Only upon deciphering the true nature of our culture and the minds and hearts of the people will we be able to discern responses that are helpful from those that would be harmful, and able to recognize responses that represent the contextualization of Christ's message from those based upon an indefensible compromise of God's Word. We must be careful to adapt to our environment in ways that establish the relevance of Christianity without going overboard in our efforts to accommodate people's needs and desires.

In closing, consider this: How well have the Christians and the Christian churches you know firsthand done in understanding cultural change? Have they responded in a strategic and professional manner?

Of course, there is still one more vital aspect of Christian ministry: What does Scripture identify as the critical, nonnegotiable principles upon which we are to build His kingdom here on earth? We will take a closer look at this in the next three chapters.

[SIX]
REVENGE OF THE GENERATION GAP

WE HAVE FIVE SIGNIFICANT GENERATIONS in America today. The names
of those segments, from oldest to youngest, are Seniors, Builders, Boomers,
Busters, and Mosaics.[1] Each segment possesses a unique set of identity factors and global perspectives.

To work most effectively with people from within each generation, it is
important to understand how they are similar and different from the other
generations, without immediately casting judgment on groups that stray
from our personal inclinations.[2]

The implications of intergenerational differences for ministry are enormous—and too often ignored. Based on extensive nationwide research, we
know that each of the four adult generations (and, one can only presume, the
Mosaics as well) tends to view the world, and especially spirituality and
churches, differently from others.

The game of life is being played differently by each new generation. The
gaps in thinking between the Boomers and the Builders and between the
Busters and the Boomers suggest that each succeeding generation is taking
greater and greater liberties at redefining the faith dimension. With most
Busters rejecting notions such as the uniqueness of Christianity, the existence of absolute moral truth, and the authority of the Bible, there are virtually no restrictions left in place to limit or guide their thinking about proper
personal or corporate spiritual development.

While the realization that most young adults have no rules or parameters
for what may be deemed acceptable or authentic spiritual growth and activity
is on one hand frightening, those who are trying to reach this generation may
use this as a license to become more aggressive and creative in the outreach of

the Church. Christians, of course, do have biblical guidelines that construct very real boundaries vis-à-vis spiritual endeavors. However, the attitudes of the emerging generations enable us to try new and bolder approaches and to reconceptualize the Church in ways that are culturally relevant while biblically appropriate. In fact, unless we exploit these new freedoms, we may lose significant opportunities to penetrate the culture.

Of course, as we try to reach younger generations with the transforming power of the gospel, we must be sensitive to the needs of those who are in the older age-groups. Builders and Seniors will never abandon the traditional church; it is difficult to give up and accept radical change in something you spent your whole life building up, particularly when you don't recognize the need for change and are unfamiliar with the alternatives.

FIVE GENERATIONS OF AMERICANS

Generation	Years of Birth	Age Range in 1998	Population Size
Seniors	1926 and earlier	72 and older	19.9 million
Builders	1927–1945	53 to 71	39.8 million
Boomers	1946–1964	34 to 52	73.1 million
Busters	1965–1983	15 to 33	72.2 million
Mosaics	1984–2002	14 and younger	61.7 million*

*total through 1997
Source: U.S. Bureau of the Census.

Most older adults are not about to accept the new ways of experiencing and learning about God. In fact, there is not much that most of them will change in terms of values, perceptions, and behaviors at this advanced state of their life.

This means that whatever form the second coming of the Church assumes, there must be provisions made to bridge the past, present, and future, recognizing the importance of the traditions, customs, and nuances of the traditional congregation to those who sustained that form throughout the past half century. We will not successfully drag most older Christians into new forms of the Church. The challenge is to enhance the existing form, which they embrace, in a way that will enable every generation to maximize spiritual growth.

Conversations about spiritual matters draw forth the variety of experiences, hopes, expectations, needs, fears, and concerns possessed by the people in these divergent segments. To discover just how different these generations are, listen to three prototypical perspectives, representing the three youngest adult segments, regarding spiritual issues. As you read these conversations, ask yourself: Is the existing church prepared to, and capable of, addressing the dreams, needs, and issues that drive the American people?

A BABY BUSTER VIEW OF THE CHURCH

Gary Knudsen is a twenty-four-year-old mired in midwestern suburbia.[3] Armed with a college degree and no real career goals, he is currently involved in computer sales.

He is still single, although he has a very active social life. He says his goal is to spend his life on a yacht, sailing from port to port across the world; he has saved no money to bring that goal to reality, nor does he have any experience sailing boats of any shape or size. He lives about forty minutes from his mother, whom he speaks to regularly by telephone. He is very pleased with this arrangement: He lives just far enough away to maximize his independence but is close enough for a quick trip home for meals, laundry, or other special experiences.

Gary was raised in a Methodist church. After a dozen years of regular, almost weekly attendance, his parents divorced, and Gary, his two younger brothers, and his mother moved to a smaller home in a different community and stopped attending church altogether. "It was a pretty sudden change, but life got pretty strange around then. It seemed like Mom was dropping all her unnecessary baggage so she could make ends meet. It was a real hard time for her; she went into survival mode. Her world became much smaller because she had to focus on what was crucial to survival. Church just wasn't one of the things she felt she needed to survive. That made an impression on me."

Once he entered high school he occasionally visited churches with friends, but his attendance—and experience—was erratic. At the University of Minnesota, though, religion was a major topic of conversation among his peers, and he was open to whatever he heard from his classmates.

Today, religion remains a major issue in his life. "I don't have a real strong church affiliation, but I'm pretty religious. I read a lot of stuff about religion, and my friends and I often talk about our beliefs and how religion affects our lives. I attend several different places. A Lutheran church, a Christian Science church, a nondenominational church, and another one that's Universalist Unity. Sometimes I go with my friends to other religious meetings, too, like one of my friends is into Islam and another is part of a Self-Realization Fellowship. It is all quite interesting and helpful. Basically I'm a Christian, but the different churches all put a different spin on religion, which broadens my thinking and helps me to clarify what I really believe and to get what I need."

Gary has both positive and negative reactions to the Christian churches he has attended over the years. "I've probably attended forty or fifty different [Christian] churches since high school.

"The thing I like about churches is the common desire that brings all those people together: They want to experience their God, and they hope to become better people as a result. The most discouraging thing is that so few people actually have that kind of supernatural encounter. It's been a frustration for me, too, especially in the Christian churches. Their emphasis is on knowing God, but then they launch into these rituals and routines, and it's been really hard for me to figure out where God is in all of that.

"Faith is kind of hard to get a grip on, but I know it's important. First of all, it's a very relational endeavor, something that should help to build bridges between people of different backgrounds. By identifying a common goal or perspective, it gives us something to work from in developing a deeper friendship. It's weird, because it's also something that's out there, you know, beyond human comprehension. It's about connecting to something more powerful, more pure, more extreme than you.

"I guess religion and faith bring very positive thoughts to my mind, like there is a reason to hope, there is some being or some force that guides things to avoid the ultimate destruction and evil."

Like most of his peers, Gary sees faith experiences as a point of common interest within his generation. The Busters are the first generation in which a majority are actively exploring non-Christian faiths and extracting core life principles from that religious potpourri; loyalty to one church, faith group, or theological system is not within their consciousness.

Their primary loyalty seems to be to a process—specifically, the process of discovery and growth. They hold spirited discussions about what they believe and how their beliefs are integrated into their lifestyles, but they are very careful not to judge the faith choices of others. To them, the process of seeking faith, truth, meaning, and purity is more important than actually arriving at an endpoint in that process. "It's a pretty cool thing because there is no right or wrong when it comes to faith. You believe what you believe, for whatever reasons seem right to you, and nobody can take that away from you. And then, if you change your mind, that's not an admission of failure or being wrong, but just a change of heart or maybe a sign that you've learned or grown. It's not like math. In spiritual matters the playing field is wide open."

Busters typically conclude that Christian churches are well intentioned but substantively lacking. Gary is no exception. "My friends and I talk about spiritual matters a lot. We feel that churches should help us handle the opportunities and anxieties that are present in our lives. But the churches we know don't do much to help shape the world, or to help us know how to cope with the problems and challenges, which we didn't ask for, and which we didn't create, but which characterize our existence and which we have to deal with. But even though churches and other religious groups haven't really satisfied our needs, we're pretty committed to spirituality. We kind of assume that every generation that came before us had the same kinds of problems with the existing outlets for religion, and they had to create systems and organizations and philosophies, which helped them cope. So we assume we'll have to do the same. It's not that big a deal to us, because we've had to re-create our reality in just about every dimension of our existence. Re-creating the church is not a big deal. Well, not to us, but it sure gets older people upset when we talk about redoing things."

Gary specifically identified a handful of typical church emphases which he and his friends find ludicrous. "They seem hung up on becoming big—you know, attracting a lot of people, as if having the biggest church means that you have something really significant. And there's always the doctrinal stuff that they think is so unique and so important. Most of the distinctions they focus on seem insignificant, stuff that has so little to do with purpose in life and making the most of your reality.

"One of the biggest stumbling blocks for my friends and me is how much most churches hate to try new things, or to experience their faith in new ways. Some of the churches I've visited get crazy over this, they go nuts over the idea of changing or doing things differently. I think it's a reflection of the dysfunctional relationships they have outside the church; they just drag their existing assumptions and limitations and fears into the church and continue to spread their dysfunctions into new realms."

One of the few times he gets angry during the discussion is when he reflects on how churches fail to involve him in their developmental process. "Man, it's like, 'Sorry, you're too young, your friends have too many earrings or strange hair, you haven't paid your dues here, young man, so you can't possibly have anything of value to add.' That really sets me off. I'm out the door at that point. Some churches won't even acknowledge your existence until you have gray hair! You aren't allowed to take part in any leadership activities, you can't get placed in any roles where you can have helpful input to shape the future. But eventually you find a few places where you can be part of the flow of ideas and relationships and contribute your piece.

"Of course, many from my generation can't find a place that allows them to contribute, so they drop out [of formal church activities] altogether. Their spiritual process takes place outside the world of churches. We're kind of used to being frozen out or ignored, so it's not ideal, but we can handle it. You just morph part of what exists into what it needs to be to become valuable."

In Gary's mind the ideal church would be built on a handful of key factors: meaningful relationships; exploratory discussions in the spiritual realm ("Don't tell me what to think, tell me the options and let me think"); down-to-earth, unpretentious people; and substantive and satisfying opportunities for involvement. "Most of my friends and I find it real hard to get connected in the churches we visit. There are too many relational barriers. For us, it's usually not worth the effort to overcome the barriers; we can have our own forms of church and spiritual growth when we get together and deal with faith issues. Sunday morning is not a sacred time to my generation."

He also touches on another matter of concern: hypocrisy. "I know it's talked about a lot, so I don't want to overdo it, but we also get real turned off by all the hypocrites. There are so many people who say they are Christian, or whatever, but who don't live the ideals their faith teaches. The world is full of manipulation, greed, dishonesty, deception. I don't need a church that's going to speak out of both sides of its mouth.

"One of the things I think my generation stands for is a higher level of genuineness. We look for that everywhere. That's why the Internet is so popular: There's no facade, it's a WYSIWYG environment."[4]

Someday Gary hopes to be married, have children, and have various aspects of his lifestyle more settled. However, he does not believe that he will lock into one church or even one faith group and park there for the duration. "Nah, faith isn't something you figure out and then cruise through life with those pieces of wisdom as your guiding light. Faith is about self-discovery and self-revelation. It's about connecting to the power that's within and the power that resides beyond your touch. You can't get too comfortable with your faith, but it shouldn't make you crazy, either.

"It's like everything else in life. You try a little of this, you try a little of that, you learn from every experience and grow. You keep on pursuing your spiritual goals, and eventually you realize that there is no right faith group, only good people trying to get along and make life worth the trip. When your faith can help you realize those kinds of life goals, then you're onto something special."

A BABY BOOMER VIEW OF THE CHURCH

It took marriage and the birth of his children to get Al Perkins back into a church. "I'd pretty much lost contact with the church during college and never saw a reason to get back into it. Peggy changed that, and for the sake of the kids I think it was a good decision."

Today Al is a vice president of marketing for a major food manufacturer in the Northeast. After completing his M.B.A., he rapidly moved up the corporate ladder, jumping from company to company every few years as better offers came along, until landing his current "prime status" position in a high-profile company.

During the course of the interview he touched upon his search for significance, his desire to make a positive difference in the world, the pressure of personal financial debt, the difficulty of sustaining true friendships, his fulfillment from his leisure pursuits, and the importance of achieving his career goals. Those are classic themes of his generation.

For the last two decades, the priority of family in his life has ebbed and flowed like the tide. When we spoke, it was during one of the high tide periods: His wife and kids were a major consideration in his decisions and emotional stability.

Now in his mid-forties (he declined to state his age), Al has had a roller-coaster experience with churches. He has gone from weekly attendance at a Catholic church during his upbringing, to total church abstinence during college and graduate school, to occasional visits to a variety of different churches (usually at the insistence of girlfriends) during his mid-twenties.

When he turned twenty-five, Al married a churchgoer; immediately after the honeymoon, the Perkinses initiated their long-running battle over church involvement. Eventually it dawned on him that with his career on a fast track, he could not have everything his way in every walk of life. Weighing the alternatives, he grudgingly acquiesced to his wife's demands, figuring the path of least resistance would provide him with leverage in their discussions related to other, more significant factors in his life.

The Perkins family has settled in at a midsize Presbyterian church, where Al's expertise in finance and marketing has landed him positions on various committees. He describes himself as a "Presbyterian Christian—you know, into organization and inclusiveness, but not real informed about theology or committed to practicing the faith." He is a member of the church, but he regards the membership as a meaningless remnant of a bygone era. "They'll take my money, my time, my talent, and my ideas, whether I'm a member or not. Membership is simply an organizational ritual used within the system for matters like determining the denominational head tax, the ego-stroking of the pastors who compare how many members they have, that sort of thing." After a pause he lightened up, adding with a laugh, "It's not like American Express. There are no privileges to membership."

Participating in a church has changed Al. "Actually, for all the crap I give my wife about it, being part of the church has had some very positive effects on me. It has allowed me to have a different level of interaction with people. At work, it's pretty savage; everyone is out for your position, for your market share. At the church, it's about as laid-back as you can imagine: There is no urgency or crisis-of-the-moment mentality; it's a very pleasant, easy environment. Sometimes it makes me crazy. But it has its advantages, I guess. The pressure is off; you don't have the same kind of standards to meet, the same sense of professionalism that you have to live up to elsewhere."

Yet, the lack of professionalism has been one of Al's hot buttons within the church. "Look, my time is valuable. I can't afford to waste it, no matter who is pushing me to be Mr. Churchman. Occasionally I get together with some of the other guys from the church for lunch or golf or whatever, and I discovered they have the same issue: The church is nice, but it just doesn't have the quality we're used to, the professionalism we'd demand elsewhere. Why should that be? And if we are supposed to be reaching other people with the gospel, how can I invite friends to events or services when I gag on the quality?

"I guess I've become one of the men who really threatens the pastor and some of his confidantes because I think what we do and the way we do it are so totally out-of-touch with the real world. I'm all for empowering people to live simpler, more fulfilling lives, but I don't think you can achieve that by stepping back in time and ignoring modern realities. I think you achieve it by resetting the rules of the game and creating space to integrate your faith views and your lifestyle.

"But I'll tell you this: Church politics is every bit as brutal and bloody as the office politics I live with in corporate America. Internal politics may be the one area where the church is more advanced than the world itself."

Al admits to having contradictory views about the church and even about Christianity. "Honestly, some of the nicest people in the world go to that church. Amazingly kind, generous, loving people. They're great role models, and I'm happy for my kids to have exposure to those people. They're usually older folks. And I really do appreciate the church's focus on spiritual things. I never had any Bible training when I was growing up, so exposure to the Bible has been very enlightening. The exhortations to get involved in spiritual behaviors, such as prayer, fasting, confession, community outreach—all of that is great stuff, and I have softened a lot over the years as a result of the teaching and activities at the church.

"But I am who I am—and frankly, sixty hours a week I am Al Perkins, vice president of marketing, a strategist, a real 'don't [expletive] with me' kind of guy. I'm the one who sees the crisis or opportunity first, creates the plan, and gets the job done. The church aggravates me because here I am, a leader in the business world, and they [the church] stick me on a committee that hasn't accomplished squat in three years; it just meets and meets and meets and meets.

"I finally figured out that I'll never be a leader in this church because real leaders threaten the pastor. He's a great guy and all, but he couldn't lead a dehydrated horse to water. So the real leaders get pushed into committees with a bunch of old-timers who despise change, and who want to relive the glory days of the church. The old guys are warm, good people, but you talk about updating the church and you see a whole different side emerge. If it weren't for Peg I'd have departed ages ago.

"You see, when you reject the things I stand for—excellence, strategic thinking, progress, efficiency, vision, controlled risks, bottom-line performance—you reject me. I used to take it personally, but I've minimized the anger by making my church involvement less of a priority.

"They want my time? They need to earn it. There's a world of great and exciting stuff waiting for me and my family. My philosophy is that the church must be able to compete. If it can't compete, then it must not have much to offer. I guess one of the hallmarks of my generation is that we can't stand compromising what's important to us simply to maintain peace and harmony with those who live in the past.

"Take something like church music. Why should I listen to choirs and organs? I never listen to them on my car radio, I never buy CDs of that stuff. The church thinks it can placate me by throwing in a few contemporary songs, but I've still got to sit through the irrelevant stuff, and that upsets me.

"Family is another one that irritates me. They talk all the time about the importance of family, family this, family that. I can't think of a single thing the church has actually done for me and my family other than make me feel guilty for not being a better father, a better husband, and a better role model. They haven't shown me how to do it—in real-world, practical terms, not in pious platitudes—and they haven't provided or described the resources I need to make it happen. So why dump on me if you can't help me?

"Another issue is the facilities. There's always some kind of building or renovation program going on that requires us to give 'above and beyond.' You know, we've got a congregation full of guys like me who are killing themselves to make their own mortgage payments, and who never have enough for the porch extension or to add a new bedroom, or to repair the busted garage door opener. The church doesn't care. I'll tell you, when you're supposed to ante up and the ante keeps growing, this permanent building campaign mentality gets old real quickly."

To Al Perkins, his future in the church is just another business decision to be made on the basis of a cost-benefit analysis. He has not determined whether he will stick with the church long-term because he knows his environment will change in a few years. "Once the kids leave home and go to college, Peg and I will enter the next phase of life. I'll be making some serious choices about my career, about our lifestyle, and about our investments at that point. How the church fits into those plans remains to be seen.

"At the moment, I can't imagine remaining as active, but we'll see how things change. God is important to me, and faith has real value in my life. Exactly how my relationship with God unfolds and how my commitment to growing as a person of faith evolves are unknowns at this stage. But I know that I am who I am. If the church continues to play the same games and to celebrate the same quality of outcomes, I would expect to see some major changes in how my religious life takes shape."

A BUILDER VIEW OF THE CHURCH

Margaret Fuller—Maggie to her friends and neighbors—has been attending Grace Baptist for nearly sixty years. "When my parents moved here they enrolled me in Sunday school, and I've been here nearly every week since then, except when we were out of town."

She comes from a long line of Baptists. Her brothers and sisters, all in their sixties and beyond, live within a day's drive, and she keeps in close touch with them. Her four children, though, are scattered throughout the country. She strives to make her house in Georgia a touchstone for the clan, but finds it exceedingly difficult. "They're all so darn independent. I guess that's good, because it's helped them handle life, but it is hard on a mother to see her children so infrequently and to realize that they never initiate these family get-togethers on their own." Although her kids range in age from thirty-three to forty, she still frets about their spiritual well-being but has "tried to leave it in God's hands. I did the best I could."

Maggie married Bill Fuller forty-one years ago. He recently retired from the construction supplies company he had served for the last twenty-eight years. One thing that becomes immediately clear about the Fullers is that they appreciate stability. Their life is characterized by longevity: same spouse, same church, same house, same community, same friends, same vacation spots, same long distance telephone company as they had more than a quarter century ago.

Familiarity and predictability bring them a sense of comfort and success. "Things change so fast these days, too fast really. I don't know how people can enjoy life when they're always trying to figure it out or change it. I know many changes are for the better, but it's unsettling to be around so much change. I think that's why so many people are dissatisfied with life and with our country these days. Their expectations are too high and they've forgotten how to settle down and enjoy the simple things in life, even if they're not perfect."

That perspective on change, quality, and fulfillment goes a long way toward understanding how Maggie views the church and faith in America today. Like so many from her generation and the generations before hers, Maggie contends that change is not always good and that the church is one place where changes often do more harm than good.

As a woman in a Baptist church, she has never held a position of leadership—nor desired one. "All the fury about whether or not women can be preachers and pastors and teachers and elders, it seems to me we've lost sight of the things that are most important. You read the Bible and you'll see that Jesus didn't spend His time teaching about women's rights. He taught about the things we need to concentrate on. And that's what the churches should be doing today, not fighting over titles and positions and power, but concentrating on whether people have trusted Jesus and whether people are reading their Bibles."

Maggie recounted the tale of a bridge club conversation she had with her friends just the week before our interview. Her three fellow players were also longtime members of Grace Baptist. "We feel bad for the pastor. How can you make sense out of all the things young people expect the church to be today? Why can't they just come and worship God and learn about Christianity so they can pass it on to their kids?

"Mary [a bridge partner] said, and I think she's right, that it hurts us when young people come in and reject the things of God that were so important to us. We know change is going to happen, and things won't stay the same forever. A lot of changes are probably necessary. But sometimes it's the way they do it that hurts the most. When they reject our traditions and customs and music and everything, they're rejecting a part of us. We created those things, or we embraced them from our parents who had created them. It's personal. We feel like we have no value in the church because the young folk are changing things so fast.

"I think it was Eleanor [another bridge partner] who said that the real problem isn't even that they change things, but that they haven't earned the right to make those changes. We poured our lives into that church and made it what it is today—made it appealing enough for those younger people to want to be part of it! But they don't respect us, they don't appreciate the history of the church, they don't realize how much we had to sacrifice to make that church what it is. Oh, the hours and hours we devoted to the church. And we contributed [money] when we really couldn't afford to, because it was the right thing to do. And now they want to shove us and our ways and some very important aspects of the Christian faith aside. It seems that they get their way because they're younger and more aggressive and they use their money as a bargaining chip."

The most significant change Maggie has experienced in the church relates to the redefinition of a successful ministry. "The emphasis upon soul winning seems gone. And the importance of building up a community of believers who will know and care for each other is also missing. We used to think of the church as a group of people who love Jesus and love each other. Not anymore. Now there's consultants and study groups and internal coalitions angling for their piece of the action, trying to redefine what's important to Jesus. How can you change what the Bible says?

"Now we have to be 'successful.' That used to mean you were obedient and submissive. Today it means you're the biggest church, with the most people, the most buildings, the most programs, the most newspaper coverage. What was wrong with the church the way it was? People knew each other, they helped and prayed for each other, they heard a good Bible message every week, they saw their neighbors get saved. Well, that's just not good enough anymore.

"You know, we had a woman in the church who was with us for forty years. She died last year and nobody from the church even knew about it until two weeks after she died. Now that never would have happened before. We always had a good visitation ministry, but now, it's just old people dying and nobody in the church is too concerned about it. I guess we represent the past, and all they care about is the future. But isn't the church supposed to be about caring for one another, about lifting each other's burdens, about loving and healing? It's hard to think of the church as part of your extended family anymore because there just isn't that kind of hospitality and nurturing and caring. It's more like church has become just another stop on each person's calendar, where we show up but we don't leave a part of ourselves there as an investment in the community of believers." One of Maggie's greatest disappointments in the church is the loss of community that she perceives. She tells stories of activities and relational networks from days past. She attributes the lost art of community to the new breed of leaders entering churches. "The young pastors coming out of seminaries, they don't know the Bible as well as they [older pastors] used to, and they spend more time on organizing and managing. That's the problem, the church has become too much like a business.

"A lot of them seem so sure of themselves, so arrogant almost. In the past, pastors were more humble. They pastored because they wanted to serve. You don't always get that same sense about today's pastors. I don't want to be judgmental, because they love Jesus and are committed to ministry, but sometimes I do wonder how things changed so much among pastors."

Organizational change is not the only shift that troubles Maggie. She is also acutely aware of the theological battles that rage in America. "People are so self-absorbed these days that they even try to make God's Word say what they want it to say. The Episcopalians are ordaining homosexuals and saying it's biblical. Most denominations accept women as preachers. You've got churches that use Bibles that say God is a 'she.' I read in our denomination's paper about new theology groups, like liberation theology, deconstruction theology, and some others I can't remember. Then there's the 'name it and claim it' movement that treats God like an ATM machine except you don't have to make any deposits, you just get unlimited withdrawals. And young people don't know the difference. They aren't spending time in the Word, so they get swept along by the newest wind. Shirley MacLaine-kinds of stuff. It's awful."

Faith is no less important to Maggie than it ever was, but her connection to the church seems a bit more tenuous. Even though she chides the young people in her congregation for hyper-personalizing faith, she admits that she, too, is guilty of making spiritual growth more of a personal than a church-related challenge. "But I'm only relying more on myself and my close friends for spiritual growth and accountability because the church just doesn't do it anymore.

"Christianity is too important for me, and too ingrained in who I am—I mean, I am sixty-four, you know—to abandon my faith and to stop growing as a Christian. The only change is that my church is no longer the center of my journey. Now I depend on myself and my friends, not because I want to but because the church doesn't really give me that option anymore.

"Don't get me wrong. I still love Grace Baptist, and they can count on me for whatever they need. But I don't know that I can count on them for whatever I need, so I'm just looking out for myself and doing what I need to so that I keep on growing. Growing old doesn't mean growing stale. I want to remain fresh and vital spiritually."

THE DEATH OF ONE-SIZE-FITS-ALL

And so we return to the challenge raised before we invaded the minds of our three cultural interpreters: Is the existing church prepared to, and capable of, addressing the dreams, needs, and issues that drive the American people?

The conversations with Gary, Al, and Maggie represent only the divergences related to age. What about those associated with racial and ethnic background? What about those driven by gender distinctions? What about the ministry implications of socioeconomic differences?

Granted, the local church in America has always served a population that harbored variety in backgrounds and expectations. But never before have we lived in a culture in which there was such an acute awareness of each group's distinctiveness. Never before have we been so capable of accessing products, services, and circumstances tailored to our needs and desires, and so impatient with situations and organizations that do not respond to our unique attributes and requirements.

The modernized language, updated music, and similar changes pioneered by seeker churches in the seventies and eighties are themselves becoming antiquated. Our society has so rapidly and completely diversified that such adaptations now seem modest and outdated, at best. Today, people seek experiences that address their needs, preferences, and expectations in a highly personalized and accessible manner. The one-size-fits-all church simply cannot compete for people's time, minds, and allegiance.

A BIBLICAL PERSPECTIVE ON
WHAT GOD EXPECTS OF HIS CHURCH

[SEVEN]
THE UNSINKABLE "TRUE CHURCH"

WHERE DO YOU START when it comes to identifying the character and disposition of the Church? Certainly, the Bible is the guidebook for the Church's calling and definition, but the entirety of the Bible is essentially the story of the development and maturation of the Church. And yet, distilling the content of the Bible into a simple picture of the Church is difficult, to say the least.

An examination of the work of biblical scholars and church leaders over the ages suggests that there is a consensus regarding the components that comprise the authentic Church of Christ, and which must be present if we are discussing the nature of the Church. These six components are known as the six pillars of the church.

THE SIX PILLARS OF THE CHURCH

The consensus indicates that there are six pillars upon which the true Church is built. Those pillars are:

1. worship

2. evangelism

3. service

4. education and training

5. building community

6. stewardship

Let's briefly examine each of these pillars as we prepare to develop a course of action that will resurrect the Church in America.

Worship

It is no accident that the first of God's Ten Commandments to His people instructs us to worship Him and Him alone.[1] Our God is one who revels in being worshiped by His creation, and His love and faithfulness to that creation over the ages certainly merit such love and obedience.

Worship is not simply an Old Testament concept, irrelevant to today's Church. The undeniable significance of worship is illustrated by the fact that just before Jesus began His public ministry, Satan attempted to derail Christ from performing His ministry by offering Jesus all the kingdoms of the world if He would simply worship Satan. Jesus was so offended by the audacity of such a request that He abruptly ended their encounter, instructing Satan to leave His presence, quoting the Scripture that tells us to "worship the Lord your God, and serve him only" (Matt. 4:8–10).

Jesus also encouraged people to focus not on peripheral aspects of worship, such as where to worship, but on the attitude of worship that true disciples possess. In the Gospel of John, Jesus dismissed one of the raging theological issues of the day by emphasizing that God is to be worshiped at all times, in all places, by those who love Him (John 4:20–24).

The apostle Paul underscored the significance of worship by exhorting believers to please God by worshiping Him, abandoning practices such as animal sacrifice and pagan rituals in favor of true worship. Paul noted that worship reflects our acknowledgment of God's perfection and power, and our willingness to be spiritually transformed by Him (Rom. 12:1–2).

In Hebrews 9 we are reminded that worship is not only an act that pleases God, but also a privilege that brings us closer to Him, and Him closer to us. In fact, our worship is to be conducted with reverence and awe, as befitting the Creator of all (Heb. 12:28).

One of the clear marks of the true Church of Christ is that it facilitates authentic and genuine worship of God, whatever form such worship may take.[2] The Bible indicates that we are to engage both in private worship, which is to occur constantly, as well as corporate worship, which would presumably occur less frequently.

The Bible outlines many ways in which corporate worship accomplishes change and growth that cannot be accomplished through private worship. Consider how God uses the musical abilities of talented musicians in leading corporate worship (see 1 Chron. 25:1–7). In the end, however, the reason we worship together is simply because God has asked us to do so, as exemplified in the experiences of Israel under the leadership of Moses, Joshua, and David. Jesus also modeled this for us by attending worship services at the local synagogue on a regular basis (see Luke 4:16). Worshiping together strengthens us as individuals while facilitating a community of believers, which we know as the Church (see 1 Cor. 14:26).

Evangelism

One of the clearest calls to the Church is found in the Great Commission, when Jesus instructed His followers to "go and make disciples of all nations" (Matt. 28:19). This was an emphatic command to His faithful ones, not an optional course of action they could choose to pursue if it pleased them.

Jesus acknowledged that evangelizing the world is a huge undertaking. But He also encouraged His followers to persevere for the sake of the numerous people earnestly seeking God who simply do not know how to connect with Him. Jesus highlighted the need for His converts to share with those seekers the good news of God's grace through Christ's love and showed the value of believers working together in their efforts to spread the gospel.[3]

Paul devoted his life to presenting the good news to people throughout the world. In his second letter to Timothy, Paul indicated that one of the great challenges to the Church is to consistently and purely communicate God's truths and expectations to people (see 2 Tim. 4:1–2).

This task was not given to a group of disconnected individuals, but to the aggregate body of Christ. Working together, we can proclaim and model the gospel to an otherwise hopeless world in a way that we could never accomplish individually. Paul described this as our ministry of reconciliation, similar to the way in which God reconciled us to Himself through the ministry and ultimate sacrifice of His Son, Jesus (2 Cor. 5:18–20). It is the task of the Church to continue the evangelistic work initiated by Jesus.

Service

All Christians are called to serve God by serving other people. We have a special responsibility to address the needs of fellow believers, as well as a permanent call to reach out to help all people both spiritually and materially. As with evangelism, our efforts at serving others are often enhanced by working in cooperation with other believers. In fact, in the book of Revelation, the church in Thyatira is praised for its acts of service to others, the good deeds done in the name of Christ.

The early church was known primarily for the way they took care of people. They certainly cared for one another's needs, sharing their wealth and possessions as necessary (see Acts 2:44–45; 4:32–34). But they also devoted themselves to serving others in ways that demonstrated their transformation and caused nonbelievers to take notice of their unusual kindness.

The Scriptures demonstrate that effective outreach is a product of a loving and compassionate heart, not simply an impersonal implementation of programs and projects. In Leviticus 19:9, God instructed the Israelites to leave behind some of each harvest for the poor to glean, a practice that enabled the indigent to feed themselves with dignity. Outreach is essentially Christian love in action—and one of the more difficult concepts for American Christians to grasp. Perhaps that is why Jesus made so many references to servanthood as the means to leadership (see Matt. 20:26).

Education and Training

Christian maturity does not happen through osmosis. People need to be taught and shown how to be Christian in thought, word, and deed. One of the critical functions of the Church is to provide exposure to God's Word and training in the application of the Word to daily circumstances.

While He was on earth, Jesus was a living example of how to equip believers for effective ministry. We read that He traveled throughout the region of Galilee to teach, to preach, and to heal. Everywhere He went, He brought with Him the leadership team He was mentoring for future responsibility, skillfully critiquing and assisting them in their forays into ministry (see Matt. 4:21; 5:7; 10:1–16; and Mark 9:28–29).

Undoubtedly that was the model that led the apostle Paul to admonish the

Thessalonians to "encourage one another and build each other up" (1 Thes. 5:11). Paul, in fact, made a career of doing just that. He was renowned for his practice of taking disciples on his ministry journeys, giving them exposure, experience, and encouragement. Among those who served their apprenticeship under his tutelage were some well-known champions of the faith, including Timothy, Titus, and Luke.

One of the greatest tasks facing the Church today is that of adequately educating and training believers so that their faith may grow to maturity. Without the equipping function in place, the Church runs the risk of becoming "a mile wide and an inch deep"—that is, having numerous people within it who identify themselves as Christian but who have no significant knowledge about their faith, and give little evidence of living its precepts.

A current example of the importance of equipping relates to evangelism. A majority of those who make a decision for Christ wander away from the church within eight weeks of making such a decision. This is largely because no one disciples or mentors those individuals as to the meaning and application of their newly embraced faith. The result is that many who make a decision never become true converts, and may be spiritually crippled for life, thinking they have mastered Christianity when, in fact, they have merely taken the first step down the road of faith. If the Church were more diligent about equipping people to understand their faith and to use their gifts and abilities to serve others, this would not happen with such horrific frequency.

Building Community

When Jesus first called His followers to be a church, He described them with the term *ekklesia*, which means an assembly of people or a group called out for a special purpose (see Matt. 16:18).

According to Christ, this assembly would be like a family, living in oneness and unity. Because God has created us with an innate need for relationships and love, the Church was intended to satisfy a portion of that longing.

Of course, the Church community is supposed to provide more than just fellowship, as important as that is. The Church fulfills other important functions as well: As a community we gather for communion and intercessory prayer and to take advantage of opportunities for confession and forgiveness. We support one another in the faith, providing encouragement through the bearing of one another's burdens, practicing mutual spiritual accountability, and sharing in the joys and hardships of the spiritual life. Indeed, one of the most compelling reasons for the assembling of the saints is to reap the promise of Jesus that when two or more are gathered in His name He will be present among them.

Stewardship

One of the tasks of the Church is to capably manage God's earthly wealth. We are to act as stewards of God's resources, returning a portion of that wealth to Him for ministry efforts.

Within ministry circles today the debate continues as to whether people are called to tithe or to present to God a heartfelt, sacrificial offering of their wealth. Likewise, church leaders debate whether resources donated for God's work should go entirely to a local church or be distributed among one or more ministries.

And yet the indisputable principle imbedded in Scripture remains constant: We are to invest a substantial portion of God's wealth in ministry. Those who love God and rely upon the Church for their spiritual growth are responsible to give generously toward its support (see Neh. 13:10; 1 Cor. 16:1–4). Stewardship goes beyond the giving of money to encompass the management of all of the resources God has entrusted to us, including our time, relationships, and skills. Ultimately, true stewardship is a reflection of righteousness, gratitude, obedience, and sensitivity.[4]

Interestingly, stewardship is also described as an act of worship, as a means to further blessing and as a means of effective outreach to the unsaved. Thus, without appropriate stewardship activity, the work of the Church is hindered and incomplete.[5]

Overall, the Church may take many forms, but for us to be the complete, healthy Church envisioned by God and defined in the Bible we must have consistent involvement in all six of these dimensions. The failure to integrate one or more of these components into our life leaves us spiritually incomplete, imbalanced, and vulnerable. The failure to invest in each of these areas concurrently renders the Church similarly weakened. Our aim must be to develop the Church in ways that weave together this rich tapestry of exhortations, examples, experiences, and emphases.

TEN IMPORTANT STEPS TO
BUILDING AN AUTHENTIC CHURCH

Knowing the pillars on which we build the Church is a necessary but insufficient condition to facilitate the emergence of the true Church. After all, the Pharisees had all the knowledge necessary to be genuine followers of God, but they did not make the grade.

Possessing an understanding of our culture and how the Church has both succeeded and failed in recent years is another necessary but insufficient condition for ministry success. What we need is a strategic framework that guides us to apply all of this knowledge and experience as we work toward achieving the outcome we seek.

Good intentions, great marketing, and an abundance of resources cannot compensate for bad strategy. If God has invested His vision for the future in our hearts and minds, we can be assured that He wants that vision to be fulfilled. However, because He has chosen to use human instruments as the means to seeing the vision come to fruition, we must operate wisely in our pursuit of His outcomes. And while it is true that we are to achieve His outcomes based upon His strength and wisdom, not our own, He has nevertheless provided us with skills and abilities that are to be used intelligently and strategically.

Strategic thinking and behavior are hallmarks of godly leaders. The Bible is filled with examples of leaders going to great lengths to devise strategic responses to their circumstances, involving God in the process through prayer, fasting, and consulting with spiritual scholars or prophets.

Joshua conducted research, prayed, and developed strategic battle plans (Josh. 8). Moses developed a layered court system, thanks to the strategic advice of his father-in-law, Jethro (Ex. 18). King Jehoshaphat snatched victory from the jaws of a military defeat by following a strategy dictated by the Lord (2 Chron. 20). King Solomon asked God for wisdom, and received it, wisely resolving a dispute between two women who claimed to be the mother of the same infant (1 Kings 3). Jesus used strategy in His response to the Jewish leaders who sought to challenge His authority, asking them to answer a question before He would answer theirs. An honest answer to His question would have been so revealing that it would have undermined the position of those who posed the original query (Matt. 21).

Before we can propose a solution to the Church's current challenge, then, what else must we take into consideration from a strategic perspective? In the preceding chapters we discussed lessons learned from past experience, some of which provided us with strategic insights that will further our quest to influence people's lives in the years to come. In addition, here are ten perspectives that should help give shape to our ultimate proposal for the second coming of the Church.

Step 1. We must have a firm and accurate understanding of our business. The railroads lost their financial footing and market share because they believed they were in the railroad business. That perception prevented them from responding strategically to the cultural and technological changes of the day. In reality, they were in the transportation business.

Similarly, many churches have lost people and missed opportunities because they have misunderstood the business they are in. Ours is not the business of organized religion, corporate worship, or Bible teaching. If we dedicate ourselves to such a business we will be left by the wayside as the culture moves forward. Those are fragments of a larger purpose to which we have been called by God. We are in the business of life transformation.

Step 2. We must know the competition for our target audience. Our competition is not other churches. Our competition is the universe of organizations, opportunities, and activities offered by the world that nudge a Christian lifestyle or Christian commitment out of the picture.

In other words, what we must create is a faith experience that is so oriented to satisfying people's felt needs at a high level of quality that the Church will successfully compete with the best that the world has to offer. Thus, if Americans are turning to people or places other than the Church, we must determine why, and then respond with a superior, faith-saturated alternative. Our alternatives will not appeal to people, though, unless we understand people and the competition for their time, attention, resources, and loyalty.

Step 3. To be effective we must anticipate, not merely react. A core principle of effective leadership is that you must try to stay one step ahead of reality. Individuals or organizations that wait until something happens, then try to devise a response, are operating at a disadvantage because they are always trailing society, never directing its path. Consequently, they have no ability to shape that society.

Alternatively, those who evaluate conditions in order to dictate or shape the future course of events are truly the influence agents of their era. Reacting to conditions is a strategy destined to achieve survival, at best. *Anticipating* conditions and preparing a course of action that directs the nature and direction of our culture allow us to change the course of history.

Step 4. Before adopting a course of action, we must consider all possible alternatives. Wisdom is not synonymous with spontaneity. Impact is not achieved by simply responding swiftly or adopting the course of least resistance or greatest popularity. The strategic individual or organization not only anticipates what is likely to happen, but also considers the alternative courses of action that might be pursued in light of the potential changes that will occur.

The most effective change agents evaluate a series of "what-if" scenarios to identify the most appropriate course of action given a set of underlying assumptions and expectations. Because every action has a consequence, wisdom demands that we reflect on the likely outcomes of all potential strategies, selecting those that promise the greatest return on our investment of resources, in light of our values and vision.

Step 5. Effective change requires a detailed plan. It has been said that those who fail to plan, plan to fail. Experience bears this out, especially in the religious realm. Reliance upon the Holy Spirit for guidance is one of the fundamental principles by which we live; but the refusal to plan ahead, sensitively, is not so much reliance upon the Holy Spirit as it is testing God.

A good plan is flexible, but it is also invaluable toward maximizing our limited resources and optimizing our efforts at reaching stated goals. A plan not only directs our efforts, but it facilitates widespread participation in, and ownership of, all efforts to enable positive transformation to occur.

Step 6. Forward movement is achieved by building upon existing strengths. Peter Drucker, the father of modern management principles and an expert in organizational strategy, is fond of saying that a core strategic principle is that you build on your strengths. The Church must identify its strengths and build upon that foundation as we restore the Church to health. Naturally, we want to improve ourselves in areas of weakness, but in the meantime, we compensate for those weaknesses by exploiting our positive attributes and abilities.

Step 7. The Church can be effective as the Church only if it operates within scriptural boundaries. We must identify the boundaries of acceptable practices for the Church. This is easier for the Church than for other entities because we have the Bible as our guidebook.

The Scriptures contain the nonnegotiable values, beliefs, and behaviors that make us the people of God. It is paramount that we obey those limitations if we are to retain our unique character and be true to our unique calling to be the Church.

Step 8. Creating a better future—the goal of vision—requires rational innovation. Innovation for its own sake is merely an exercise in creative disruption. Our task is to grasp and articulate God's vision for our future and to facilitate the change necessary to create that future. But not all change is acceptable; we must establish parameters as to what is success and failure, what is good and bad.

In the course of creating positive change, we will have to take risks, but the effective individual or organization pursues only those risks that are integral to the desired outcomes, and that can be logically and reasonably defended.

Step 9. Success demands that we think holistically. Organizations and individuals that make alterations without regard to the "big picture" run the risk of introducing change that is either counterproductive or inconsequential.

The ones who make a lasting difference in people's lives (and therefore in our society) are those who assess the broader implications of those changes: What other individuals or groups will this change affect? How does it fit into our organization's long-term goals? Are those being affected by this change being included in the process of implementing the change? Have we realistically measured the demands on existing resources? Is this the best course of action, given all these factors?

As Scripture tells us, the Christian life is a marathon, not a sprint, so we must be prepared for a long-term effort. To sustain and to maximize such an effort requires that we conceive our actions in light of God's kingdom, not merely our personal fiefdom.

Step 10. Lean not on your own understanding. For several decades, the Church has relied upon greater sums of money, better techniques, bigger numbers and facilities, and more impressive credentials as the means to influence society at large. These elements have failed us; in our efforts to serve God, we have crowded out God Himself.

It is important to remember that God does not need us to accomplish any of His ends, yet He has chosen to work through us. We must be constantly sensitive to His guidance, which He gives to us through the Bible, experience, history, and direct revelation.

Remember that the struggle to revitalize the Church is a spiritual battle. As fallible, fallen humans, we are in over our heads. We can certainly use the gifts, skills, experiences, and resources that God provides for our efforts to fight the good fight of faith, but we must also remember that left to our own devices and capabilities, we will surely lose ground. We cannot make progress without the lordship and influence of God.

[E I G H T]
WHAT DOES A REAL LEADER LOOK LIKE?

JESUS MUST EXPERIENCE a sense of déjà vu as He surveys the American church today. It was just two millennia ago that He ministered among the people of Israel and felt His heart sink in sadness. "When he saw the crowds, he had compassion on them, because they were harassed and helpless, like sheep without a shepherd" (Matt. 9:36).

This verse is a vivid image of the Church today: millions of people busily engaged in meaningless activity in a vain attempt to find purpose, direction, and comfort, but pitifully mired in chaos and confusion. It is neither the condition God intended for us, nor a necessary state of affairs.

The Church is paralyzed by the absence of godly leadership. Our leadership vacuum can be attributed to a number of factors:

- Many churches dismiss the importance of leadership;
- Many of us misunderstand the nature of leadership;
- Many refuse to adequately identify, nurture, and support those whom God has called to lead.

The good news is that God has provided us with the leaders needed to guide the Church forward in these days of turbulence and challenge. If we can clarify our notions about leadership and enable leaders to lead, the Church will be a much healthier body of people, and have a much greater impact on our society.

WHY ARE LEADERS NECESSARY?

In working with pastors and church leaders across the nation, I have been amazed by the numbers who dismiss the importance of leadership.

Naturally, those who question the significance of having a competent and godly leader to guide the people shroud their argument in holy-speak: "Leaders are not critical to the health of the Church. As long as we preach the Word of God and commit ourselves to living in faith, He will take care of us."

While that kind of reasoning might appeal to some, it is both naive and intrinsically harmful. Granted, we must preach the Word of God, for it is only by hearing the truth about God's holiness, our sinfulness, and Jesus' atoning death and resurrection that people can be restored into a proper and lasting relationship with God (see 2 Tim. 4:2). It is also true that we must commit ourselves to holy living, so that we may please God, enhance the quality of our own lives, and attract others to follow Jesus. And certainly God wants to take care of those who long to be His devoted followers.

But how do you think God plans for us to deal with the bigger challenges and complexities of life? Scriptural evidence reveals that He expects us to defeat darkness by working together. God allows us to face obstacles and temptations in order to build character in us as individuals and strengthen us as members of His body. He expects us to rely upon each other as we strive to do His work in a world that is often skeptical or outright hostile to His ways and His expected outcomes.

To effectively achieve His ends, God has provided not only a community to get the job done, but also special abilities known as spiritual gifts. Those gifts enable us to minister beyond our levels of natural competence and ability in order to meet the needs of the Church.[1]

GIFTS ENOUGH FOR ALL

God has provided each believer with at least one spiritual gift or gifts; it is our responsibility to use whatever gift He provides for the good of the Church. In Romans 12:6–8, Paul explores some of these gifts:

> We have different gifts, according to the grace given us. If a man's gift is prophesying, let him use it in proportion to his faith. If it is serving, let him serve; if it is teaching, let him teach; if it is encouraging, let him encourage; if it is contributing to the needs of others, let him give generously; if it is leadership, let him govern diligently.

Notice that not all teachers are considered leaders—that is a separate gift. I emphasize this point to emphasize that just because someone—say, a senior pastor—is a gifted teacher, that does not automatically make him a gifted leader. Each of us has been gifted by God, as He sees fit, to fulfill a specific role within the Church.

Remember, no single gift is better than any other gift, nor is one believer superior to any other, because of the specific gift that has been entrusted to him or her. In 1 Corinthians 12:14, Paul compares the body of Christ to a human body, with each part of the body needing to fulfill its unique and necessary function. Similarly, without leaders providing direction, vision, and counsel (the "brains" of that body), the productivity of the whole group declines.

God's intent is that we each use our gifts in ways that complement the gifts bestowed upon other believers, living with and ministering to each other in unity, to achieve God's will for the Church. When Christians deny the importance of the gift of leadership, that denial has three effects.

First, it diminishes the standing of those who possess a gift from God. This elevates the person who is rejecting the significance of leadership above the person gifted as a leader. This is unacceptable; we are all equal in Christ, and we have been called to use our gifts cooperatively, toward the furtherance of His kingdom.

The importance of using our gifts as unifying resources toward building the Church is outlined in 1 Corinthians 3:5–9:

> What, after all, is Apollos? And what is Paul? Only servants, through whom you came to believe—as the Lord has assigned to each his task. I planted the seed, Apollos watered it, but God made it grow. . . . For we are God's fellow workers.

The early Church was being divided by contentious individuals who had placed their ultimate allegiance with men rather than God. In this passage, Paul reminded them to remember the Source of the gifts, rather than putting too much stock in the giftings or opinions of one individual.

Second, downplaying the importance of leadership paralyzes the Church by removing a crucial ability from the mix of abilities that are necessary for the Church to be healthy, functional, and growing.

Third, rejecting or minimizing the leadership gift—and those who possess the gift—insinuates that we know better than God when it comes to planning and preparing for the future of His Church. The Bible offers story after story of the trials and tribulations of God's people, but He always provided them with a gifted leader to show the way. In every period of Church history, God has used great leaders as key people for the development of the Church. Moses, Joshua, David, Nehemiah, Peter, and Paul are just a few of the leaders whom God ordained to lead.

In postbiblical times, the list of high-profile leaders serving the needs of the Church is long, ranging from Constantine and Gregory to Martin Luther and John Wesley, to more contemporary Church leaders such as Martin Luther King, Chuck Colson, Bill Bright, Bill Hybels, and Bill McCartney. Every leader whom God has ever chosen was a sinner, but they all have possessed a passion for God, a desire to live a holier life, and a commitment to help God's people get closer to Him.

Because God's principles always work, regardless of the context in which they are applied, the importance of leadership can be seen even outside the realm of the Church. Every successful movement or revolution that has taken place in the past four hundred years has had a strong, visionary leader pointing the way. Just as the Church has leaned on the courage, wisdom, and direction of those God selected as His leaders, so through the ages have groups of people seeking change and influence turned to individuals who could articulate vision, attract followers, develop a strategic direction, and encourage people to work together toward the fulfillment of their dreams. Those individuals are true leaders—and their leadership is indispensable.

FOLLOW THE LEADER

If God has gifted certain individuals as leaders, and not all leaders are pastors, why are they not stepping forward to take their God-given place? There are four primary reasons why most Americans avoid positions of leadership.

First, leadership is hard work. Making tough and sometimes unpopular decisions takes a tremendous amount of courage. Leaders must devise wise strategies, often in situations that are complex and involve rapidly changing variables. In our interviews with people throughout the nation, many said that a person would be crazy to try leading others unless that person truly felt called or gifted as a leader. Only one out of every four people believe that others view them as a leader. And only about one out of every ten adults demonstrate leadership ability to any significant extent.

Second, leading people carries huge responsibility. People's lives are often dramatically influenced by the choices a leader makes, and those in leadership must be prepared to answer for the outcomes of those choices. In a society that treasures entertainment, pleasure, comfort, and popularity, seeking a position of leadership is not always perceived to be the "smart" choice.

Third, relatively few people have been prepared for leadership responsibilities. The education we typically receive equips us for tasks that are more cut and dried: managing, repairing, designing, teaching, selling, and so on. Effective leadership requires some expertise in a broad range of areas, including psychology, marketing, management, sociology, communications, education, finance, philosophy, and human relations.

Leadership is an art, not a science. While leaders are born, not made, assuming leadership duties without proper training, development, and experience can result in disastrous outcomes, for both the leader and the followers.

Fourth, leadership requires a compelling vision of a future that people will seek to pursue. Developing a compelling vision is a hallmark of a great leader, and it is the point of initiation in anyone's leadership. Without a compelling vision that unleashes the passion and excitement of both leaders and followers, leadership becomes simply a process of maintaining the status quo.

WHAT DOES A REAL LEADER LOOK LIKE?

If those who are supposed to lead the Church are not always the pastors of individual churches or ministries, and leaders won't automatically step forward and identify themselves, how are we to recognize them?

First, we must know what to look for. There are as many definitions of leadership as there are people seeking to define this ability. When we say that someone has the gift of leadership, what does that mean?

One definition that is commonly used in church circles originated with J. Oswald Sanders: "Leadership is influence."[2] But this definition leaves much to be desired. When you teach facts or principles to someone, you may influence his or her thinking, but you are not necessarily practicing leadership.

This confusion between the role of teaching and the role of leadership has made it difficult for many pastors, who are trained and gifted to teach, to understand why they are ineffective in facilitating progress toward the achievement of a God-given vision. For our purposes, the good generic definition of leadership is as follows:

> A leader is someone who effectively motivates, mobilizes resources, and directs people toward the fulfillment of a jointly embraced vision.[3]

Leadership is about motivating people to behave at specific times in certain ways for prescribed ends. It entails mobilizing groups of people to achieve ends that cannot be accomplished by a single expert. Leadership identifies and accesses the resources necessary to accomplish the desired outcomes. It provides sufficient direction so that people's resources are used effectively and efficiently.

The unifying thread among these elements is that these efforts are made in pursuit of the fulfillment of a common vision. Without a clear vision, there is no place to lead people. Without vision, chaos ensues, entropy escalates, and a sense of aimlessness prevails, no matter how charismatic or brilliant the leader may be.

For the Church to exert a positive influence in our culture, we need leaders who are able to give reluctant and busy people a vision for the future that will make them want to get involved in the things of God. We need leaders who can orchestrate efforts that result in life transformation for the glory of God and the good of His creation; this involves pointing them to the resources needed to get the job done, and providing plans and guidance to those who have heeded the call to know, love, and serve God.

Future leaders of the Church will need to expend themselves in the endless pursuit of the vision for life transformation within our culture, a vision God Himself has given them to disseminate to the Church.

THE THREE C'S OF CHRISTIAN LEADERSHIP

Now that we have introduced a general, working definition for leadership, we must take it to the next level in order to define what we mean by the term "Christian leader."

Being a leader of God's people is a higher and more significant calling than being a leader in business or government. All leaders are important, but leading for God is a special, unique privilege. Toward that end, we may use the following as a definition of a Christian leader:

> A Christian leader is someone who is called by God to lead and possess virtuous character and effectively motivates, mobilizes resources, and directs people toward the fulfillment of a jointly embraced vision from God.

Often we fall into the trap of perceiving leaders to be people who have risen to prominence largely because they possess special gifts in communication or problem solving. Such a view is unjust to leaders. Usually they are complex, multifaceted beings. Christian leaders possess a unique blend of three special elements:

1. *calling* or anointing;
2. godly *character;* and
3. leadership *competencies.*

If any one of these elements is absent, the individual may not be a leader and, if turned loose to lead, may cause irreparable harm through their ill-advised attempts to lead.

Let's take a closer look at each one of these "leadership essentials."

CALLING

God's calling is the necessary starting point in the life of a leader. There is absolutely no substitute. In other words, if you have not been called by God to lead His people, do not seek to do so on the basis of your own abilities or desire. Leaders are called to serve and they serve by leading—not by forcing their will upon the people, but by becoming the connection between the past, present, and future in ways that bring God and His people into closer relationship.

There are three primary levels of leadership: within families or other small groups (micro-leadership); within churches or other local organizations (mezzo-leadership); and those roles with the widest reach and highest level of responsibility and visibility (macro-leadership).

The scope of leadership God expects most people to provide does not extend beyond their immediate family. However, those who have been called by God to higher levels of leadership are provided with discernible signs of this calling.

Eight Signs of God's Call to Leadership

In my observation of leaders at all three levels, there appear to be eight indicators of God's calling to leadership. I have noticed that the called possess most, if not all, of these signs. These signs are readily identifiable in both Scripture and contemporary ministry.

1. *Leaders have an awareness of God's call.* People whom God calls are generally sensitive to that calling. While there is sometimes a tendency to fight or deny the call, the Holy Spirit is persistent, producing a mounting and undeniable pile of evidence that He has chosen you to serve as a leader.

2. *Leaders possess an inclination to lead.* Whether this is manifested in a very undeniable urge to lead or in a nagging sense of the necessity to lead, leaders cannot help themselves. When they are in the presence of a group that requires leadership, they will inevitably gravitate toward that position. Asking a leader not to lead is like telling a mother not to love her newborn child—it just won't happen!

3. *Leaders perceive reality differently from non-leaders.* Leaders often perceive reality differently from other people; they reach different conclusions

regarding the environment and react to conditions and opportunities differently. They are analytical, whether based on an intuitive feel for a situation or on empirical information. They are strategic in their assessment of matters. They are future-focused, always building mental bridges between the present and the future. They are visionaries, frequently ignoring the details in favor of the big picture. If an individual cannot identify and articulate God's vision for the ministry he or she has been called to lead, then that individual certainly is not a leader. True leaders are change agents, willing to take risks if they are reasonable and if they can produce significant returns.

4. *Leaders naturally influence people.* One of the marks of a leader is the influence that person has in the lives of people. Leaders use all available means to impact the vision, perceptions, values, attitudes, beliefs, relationships, and lifestyle choices of the people with whom they have contact. Just as a person may partially determine a call by seeing if anyone is following them, so may we discern a calling to lead by ascertaining if people experience transformation through their interaction with the potential leader.

5. *Leaders seek each other out as companions.* People like to be around others like themselves because there is a natural camaraderie and similarity of worldview. They share an understanding of the same issues, challenges, obstacles, joys, frustrations, and dreams that get their minds racing and their hearts pounding. If you want to develop a comfort zone for the typical leader, put him or her in the presence of other leaders; they will quickly sense a kinship with their fellow leaders.

6. *Leaders receive external acclaim.* Since most Americans are followers by nature, when a true leader emerges, people feel more relaxed about life and more excited about the future. Consequently, people tend to affirm the gifts of a leader. The most significant affirmation, however, is that received from other true leaders. When they sense one of their own, there is a tendency to affirm the newly identified leader. While leaders are often highly competitive individuals, they know a leader when they encounter one.

7. *Leaders possess internal strength.* Leadership is not easy. Among the key elements required for effective leadership are self-confidence and courage. Such strength is manifested in championing the tough, unpopular stands; taking risks; penetrating uncharted waters; accepting responsibility for judgment calls; resolving tensions and conflicts; and persevering in the face of discouraging odds. Merely casting and maintaining a vision from God takes a certain level of fortitude that most people never muster.

8. *Leaders derive joy from leading.* Even though leadership is often a headache a minute, leaders wouldn't be caught dead stifling their leadership gifts. The headaches are simply the price that must be paid en route to greater achievement and intensified fulfillment. True spiritual leaders wouldn't trade all the security in the world for the thrill of taking people to a higher plane of accomplishment and spiritual growth.

CHARACTER

One of the signs of the ability to be a Christian leader is godly character. Leaders are not perfect by any stretch of the imagination; we are all fallen creatures who continue to sin and make mistakes. However, leaders maintain the heart of David, who was described as being a man after God's own heart (see 1 Sam. 13:14). Since leaders are people who facilitate life transformation and whose own lives often serve as the example for others, what more appropriate nature would God choose for His leaders than that they exhibit the personal qualities that He esteems?

The simplest way of defining the desired character of leaders is to say that they are to be like Jesus Christ. But we all fall short of that goal! It may be helpful to notice some of the traits found in biblical leaders that are of the greatest value in leading.

The following table lists some of those attributes that are readily identifiable in the great leaders portrayed in the Bible (for example, Abraham, Noah, Moses, Joshua, Joseph, David, Nehemiah, Paul, and Peter). Notice that these are not qualities meant to be unique to leaders, but are the very same characteristics that every Christian is called to demonstrate.

Godly character is a prerequisite to Christian leadership because the actions of a leader flow from his or her innate qualities. The types of decisions leaders make spring from their courage, sensitivity, values, compassion, vision, and discernment. Their ability to resolve conflict is a direct reflection of their perseverance, courage, sense of fairness, self-control, and trustworthiness. People are motivated by a leader not just because of a compelling vision that is artfully communicated, but also by the sense of the leader's desire to serve, high integrity, appropriate values, consistency, and wisdom. When leaders experience longevity in service, it is attributable to their energy, faithfulness, loyalty, passion, reliability, integrity, and courage as much as it is to their productivity and political skills.

THE CHARACTER QUALITIES OF A GODLY LEADER

honesty	energetic
loyalty	faithfulness
perseverance	self-controlled
trustworthiness	loving
courage	wise
humility	discerning
sensitivity	encouraging
teachability	patient
optimism	passionate
even-temperedness	fairness
joy	merciful
gentleness	reliability
consistency	servant's heart
spiritual depth	values-driven
forgiveness	compassion

Because God is more interested in who we are than in what we do, character takes center stage in determining the suitability of a person for spiritual leadership. Indeed, one of the central means through which a leader directs people is through his or her character: It is an example for others to follow.

The individuals in Scripture who served as leaders but eventually became disqualified for their responsibilities lost their privileged position not because of incompetence but because of rotten character. Saul had great ability but lacked integrity, fortitude, and self-control. Laban was undermined by his selfishness, deceitfulness, and arrogance. Reuben lacked courage, consistency, and passion.

On the other hand, God sometimes uses leaders in spite of the fact that they don't have pristine characters. After all, God used Moses in mighty ways despite Moses' history as a murderer. Israel is said to be the nation of Jacob even though he stole his own brother's birthright. God is able to use us in spite of our faults and weaknesses, as long as we have a commitment to become people of Christian character.

COMPETENCIES

Being called to lead, possessing a clear vision for the future, and being a person of righteous character are indelible marks of a leader. However, unless the individual possesses certain basic leadership skills, the leader is impotent.

A person is not a teacher because he or she has great knowledge and hopes to transfer that information to others. A teacher is one who has successfully transmitted useful facts and processes to students so that they are better informed and more capable than before they encountered the teacher. Similarly, leaders are known by the products of their efforts; true leaders possess various skills and abilities that enable them to get results.

The leader's chief skills revolve around the core aims of the leader: motivating, mobilizing, resourcing, and directing people in the pursuit of a vision from God. The leader must have an abundance of resources available in order to make things happen, whether the desired outcomes relate to strategic planning, conflict resolution, group motivation, resource development, creating a corporate culture, or directing the activities of team leaders.

No leader, of course, possesses perfect abilities in all of the areas shown in the accompanying chart of leader competencies, but effective leaders are sufficiently skilled in each of these areas to do what must be done to facilitate life transformation, and continue to hone their skills so that they might become even more effective. Every leader usually shines most brightly in one specific aspect of leadership, an aspect we will describe as his or her "dominant aptitude."

THE FUNCTIONAL COMPETENCIES OF A CHRISTIAN LEADER

- Identifying, articulating, and conveying God's vision
- Motivating people to be supportive and involved
- Developing and coaching people to reach their full potential
- Synthesizing volumes of information to make strategic decisions
- Persuading people to do what's right, in light of the vision
- Engaging in strategic thinking, initiating strategic action
- Spearheading conflict resolution
- Developing the resource base
- Effectively communicating truths, principles, and plans
- Delegating authority and responsibility
- Reinforcing people's commitment to the vision and the group
- Celebrating successes achieved
- Making key decisions
- Building a team of people with shared purpose and complementary gifts
- Initiating evaluation of needs, plans, opportunities, procedures, and outcomes
- Creating a viable corporate culture
- Maintaining people's focus and priorities
- Instituting reasonable methods and standards of accountability
- Modeling godly behavior and values
- Directing the efforts of other key leaders in the group

The dominant aptitude of a leader is like an area of specialization; it represents the specific aspect of leadership in which the individual truly stands head and shoulders above even other gifted and called leaders. Let's consider the variety of aptitudes that leaders may possess.

FOUR TYPES OF LEADERSHIP

I believe there are four types of leaders.[4] In the most effective organizations, movements, and systems, all four types of leaders are present, working in unison toward the achievement of the vision. The absence of any one of these types renders the movement unstable and incomplete—not impotent, but not operating at full capacity, either. The types are the Directing Leader, the Team-Building Leader, the Strategic Leader, and the Operational Leader.

1. The Directing Leader

This is the individual who provides the spark. The Directing Leader (DL) is the visionary force in the ministry, constantly reminding people of the unique calling God has given them as an entity, and motivating people to deepen their commitment to that vision. The DL is uniquely gifted as a catalyst, defining the cause to which people will devote themselves. He defines not only the vision, but also the values that relate to the vision. He also dictates the standards of performance to which the group must rise. The DL is passionate about the vision, and infects others with that same sense of significance and urgency of the vision.

Because a Directing Leader is more of a "big picture" person than a detail person, it is imperative that this person be surrounded by other leaders who are competent with the details of converting vision into reality. Directing Leaders are often so focused on the vision that they can seem insensitive to those who are curious about the vision or who wish to be personally nurtured in understanding and participating in the cause. Their single-mindedness sometimes undermines their ability to motivate people to get involved.

LEADERSHIP STYLES AND EMPHASES

Dominant leader	Focus	Currency	Unique attributes, strengths	Weaknesses	Products
Directing leader	vision	ideas	catalyst; values-driven; visionary; standards; passion; motivation; independent; assertive	details; sensitivity; hate compromise; impatient; dictatorial; too talkative; self-centered	purpose; vision; recruits
Strategic leader	analysis	information	wisdom; synthesis; testing; reflection; patience; thorough; pragmatic; well-prepared	people skills; perfectionism; internalize emotions	plans; new programs
Team-building leader	mobilizing	communication	relationships; blending talents; tactful; enthusiastic; optimistic; flexible	details; too emotional; can become disorganized; misuses time	teams
Operational leader	managing	structure	organized; creates process and order; supportive; accurate; efficiency; focused; details	vision; insensitivity; lacks enthusiasm; too cautious	efficiency; systems

No ministry can be successfully launched without a Directing Leader identifying and casting the vision, recruiting followers, and keeping those followers pumped up about the reason for which they have assembled. As a ministry matures, the Directing Leader may lose some of the limelight since other aspects of the ministry will naturally assume a higher profile. However, even though the Directing Leader may lose center stage within the ministry, there is no time in the life of any ministry when it can afford to be without his effective leadership. Someone must always play this vital role if the heartbeat of the organization and its future focus are to remain intact and healthy.

2. The Team-Building Leader

The primary contribution of the Team-Building Leader (TBL) is the ability to mobilize people to pursue the vision. This individual is adept at organizing and communicating for the completion of tasks. The TBL orchestrates the different talents and abilities of those involved to establish a coordinated, comprehensive team committed to working together for a common purpose.

The most effective TBLs have an innate gift for blending people into productive, functioning units. While the Directing Leader is able to persuade people to get involved because the vision is so compelling, the Team-Building Leader moves those recruits into relationships and capacities that maximize their personal abilities and gifts toward the greater end. These leaders are highly relational and take great pleasure in seeing people revel in their productivity.

3. The Strategic Leader

Directing Leaders tend to be intuitive in their decision-making style. Strategic Leaders (SL) are the flip side of the coin; they provide the empirical analysis of situations and opportunities to develop a well-researched and carefully conceived strategy for action. They create plans that outline the details of future action, incorporating the vision cast by the Directing Leader and the human resources mobilized by the Team-Building Leader.

Strategic Leaders are less swayed by the emotional seduction of the vision than they are by the tangible potential of the vision. They use their keen insight into people and circumstances to develop clever approaches to doing the impossible. You can imagine how powerful a duo a Directing Leader and a Strategic Leader would be: Between them, they cover the bases when it comes to envisioning, conveying, and planning for the development of a different, superior future.

As a consequence of synthesizing information and opportunities into a fine-tuned plan for the future, the Strategic Leader is also effective at identifying and accumulating the resources necessary to get the job done. It often takes the gifts of the Directing Leader to "close the sale" (for example, to gain a large donation, to persuade a skilled individual to join the team, or to cajole a reluctant real estate developer into working with a ministry). Often, however, it was the shrewd sensitivities and creative thinking of the SL that facilitated those victories.

4. The Operational Leader

The Operational Leader (OL) is the managing partner in the leadership team. These people have managerial abilities, although they have the calling, the gifting, and the capabilities of a true leader. They are "hyper-managers"— able to do management tasks, but performing those duties with the mind and heart of a leader. Like a manager, they are able to devise systems that will make the entire ministry run smoothly, but they can do so without depleting the life brought to the ministry by a focus on the vision.

Operational Leaders emphasize the value of efficiency. They develop procedures that empower, rather than rules and policies that limit. Their primary concern is to create a ministry operation in which the ministry units developed by the Team-Building Leader are able to carry out the plans devised by the Strategic Leader in pursuit of the vision articulated by the Directing Leader.

The OL is often a faceless, little-known individual. The DL is invariably high profile, center stage, and associated with the very heart of the ministry. The TBL is the most popular of the leaders, given his investment in understanding people and knitting them together in fulfilling and effective ministry endeavors. The SL is recognized as "the brains" of the outfit, frequently working behind the scenes to prepare a major initiative for public presentation and deployment. The OL is the one who fits all the pieces together at the grass-roots level, using the skills of managers, counselors, teachers, helpers, and anyone else who is attracted by the vision to ensure an efficient delivery of ministry products and services.

In the most effective ministries, all four types of leaders are present and working in harmony. In ministries that lack one or more of those types, it sometimes happens that the existing leaders are expected to assume the responsibilities of the missing leader-types. While this is theoretically logical, most leaders are gifted in one or two areas; it is the rare individual who can capably fill three or four of those leadership dimensions.

An alternative is to delegate specific functions typically addressed by the absent leader-type to an individual who has strengths in a particular aspect of what that leader does. For instance, if a Directing Leader is absent, the motivational function may be carried by a particularly gifted teacher, who can inspire people to commit to the vision.

The least effective, but most commonly embraced, alternative is for the ministry to simply do the best it can without the missing leader-type. There will be gaps in the ministry's efforts, and people may be somewhat confused by what takes place. However, if the dominant leader determines that positive transformation will take place to such an extent that continuation is justifiable, then the ministry may choose to move ahead, praying all the while that God will bring forward the missing leader.

In closing, let me note that over 70 percent of the Protestant churches in America today have only one full-time employee—the Senior Pastor. The notion of having four major leaders in a ministry may seem absurd, since most churches could not possibly afford such a team of stalwarts. However, not every ministry leader needs to be a full-time, paid professional.

There is a growing list of churches across the nation where the leaders are emerging from the congregation and are serving in a volunteer or bi-vocational capacity. Neither seminary degrees nor formal titles have anything to do with being called by God to lead. As we prepare for the second coming of the Church, we must become more adept at recognizing latent gifts of leadership, and doing what we can to help potential leaders cultivate their gifts for the good of the entire Church.

[NINE]
THINKING LIKE A CHRISTIAN

WHEN I WAS IN GRADUATE SCHOOL, one of my part-time jobs was working for a glass and aluminum company. Our job was to replace broken windows, install shower enclosures and new window units, and repair auto windshields.

Nothing in my past had remotely prepared me for the demands of this job. My wife, who knows that I am perhaps the least mechanically inclined man in the Northern Hemisphere, predicted a rough transition for me from the white-collar world to the blue-collar world. She didn't know the half of it. Within one week both my mind and my body were reeling from severe culture shock. Indeed, my wife used to marvel at the number of cuts and bruises I'd accumulate in the course of eight hours at work.

My first six months were spent apprenticing under the tutelage of a master glazier who seemed to know everything there was to know about glass, aluminum, home repairs, and anything mechanical. (My areas of expertise—urban development, statistical analysis, electoral politics, survey sampling, and design—failed to impress him.) He had enormous patience and attempted to teach me everything he knew.

In fact, it didn't take long for me to learn three very important lessons. First, I discovered that if you do not have the right team of people working together, you cannot get the job done properly. Second, if you do not have the right tools, no amount of ingenuity or goodwill can compensate for that deficiency. (The third lesson, more personal in nature, was that I desperately needed to get a different job; my life and that of my coworkers was jeopardized every time I tried to remove a piece of broken glass or to install a new piece. The brethren at the glass shop wholeheartedly endorsed my decision to seek other means of paying my tuition bill.)

Those same lessons—well, the first two, anyway—are pertinent to the condition and future of the American church. Until we can develop unity based on a shared vision, a common purpose, and consensual beliefs, the Church will struggle to influence its own people, much less those who are on the outside looking in. And, of course, if the people composing the Church have not been adequately prepared to engage in the struggles that will always confront the true Church, then the chances of achieving success in those struggles are severely diminished.

If our goal as believers is to be fully obedient to God, and to become change agents in society through our collective commitment to His principles, our first pursuit must be to ensure that we as Christians have a mental framework that leads us to view the world through a Christian lens.

BUILDING A "BIBLICAL WORLDVIEW"

People tend to respond to each experience, relationship, piece of information, and opportunity on the basis of their frames of reference. These perspectives, which are composed of our beliefs and values, affect the way we view the world around us. Cumulatively, they constitute a person's worldview.

Our worldview impacts every aspect of our lives—how we spend our time and money, how we interact with other people in public and private, how we order our priorities, and even how we perceive God. Jesus' life on earth was geared to restoring us to spiritual wholeness so that our thoughts reflect God's priorities and principles. We refer to this as having a "biblical world-view." Those who have a biblical worldview have different priorities and respond to situations differently from those who have an existentialist or materialistic worldview. At least, that is how it should be.

IT'S TIME FOR A REALITY CHECK

The Bible clearly states that true believers should be readily distinguished from nonbelievers by the way they live. Yet, the evidence undeniably suggests that most American Christians today do not live in a way that is quantifiably different from their non-Christian peers, in spite of the fact that they profess to believe in a set of principles that should clearly set them apart. We tend to rely upon a cultural filter rather than a biblical filter for interpreting daily events, information, experiences, and opportunities.[1]

Examples of the Similarity of Attitudes Between Christians and Non-Christians

Behavior	Born-again Christians	Non-Christians
Feel completely or very successful in life	58%	49%^^
Describe yourself as "a fundamentalist"	28%	23%^
It's impossible to get ahead because of your financial debt	33%	39%**
Your religious beliefs actually change the way you behave	92%	74%**
You are still trying to figure out the purpose of your life	36%	47%**
You feel you are an outstanding role model for young people	80%	69%**
Family is most responsible for teaching forgiveness to kids	90%	81%*
Satisfied with your life these days	69%	68%"
Your personal financial situation is getting better	27%	28%"

Sources:
* OmniPoll 2-97, July 1997, N=1012, Barna Research Group, Ltd., Oxnard, CA.
** OmniPoll 1-97, January 1997, N=1007, Barna Research Group, Ltd., Oxnard, CA.
^ OmniPoll 2-96, July 1996, N=1018, Barna Research Group, Ltd., Oxnard, CA.
^^ OmniPoll 1-96, January 1996, N=1004, Barna Research Group, Ltd., Oxnard, CA.
" Donor Compass 97-2, August 1997, N=1087, Barna Research Group, Ltd., Oxnard, CA.

Let's think about this for a minute. If a Christian is someone whose life has been radically touched by God, and is indwelled by the Holy Spirit, how is it possible for that person to experience and respond to reality the same as non-Christians do? The answer is simple but devastating.

Most Christians have plentiful exposure to God's truths and exhortations, but few have actually been pierced by the truth, principles, and meaning of the Christian faith.

Most Christians—and I'm talking about individuals who have made a clear profession of faith in Jesus Christ as their Savior and sole means of salvation—do not seem to understand the nature of the commitment they allegedly have made to become devoted followers of Christ. Since the Christian Church has largely divorced evangelism from discipleship, believers are comfortable with relying upon Jesus Christ for their spiritual salvation—and upon themselves for everything else.[2]

We have been exposed to sermons that challenge us to "lean on Jesus," Bible verses that encourage us to turn to God for direction and strength, and hymns that proclaim a reliance on God's power and protection. But to the average Christian, these are empty, even perplexing, platitudes. In order to reverse this trend, we must allow the life-changing truths of the gospel to reach into the inner core of our minds and hearts. Only then will we be credible witnesses to the power of Christ's transforming love to those around us.

THE GENESIS OF THE PROBLEM

If you dig a bit beneath the surface, the core reason why so few Christians possess a biblical filter on reality becomes apparent. The vast majority of Christians do not behave differently because they do not think differently, and they do not think differently because we have never trained them, equipped them, or held them accountable to do so.

For years we have been exposing Christians to scattered, random bits of biblical knowledge through our church services and Christian education classes. They hear a principle here and read a truth there, then nod their head in approval and feel momentarily satisfied over receiving this new insight into their faith. But within the space of just a few hours that principle or truth is lost in the busyness and complexity of their lives. They could not capture that insight and own it because they have never been given a sufficient context and method that would enable them to analyze, categorize, and utilize the principle or truth.[3]

This inability to systematically apply scriptural truth produces a spiritual superficiality or immaturity that is reflected in behavior. For example, the average Christian spends more time watching television in one evening than he or she spends reading the Bible during the entire week. Only four out of ten people who claim to be Christian also claim they are "absolutely committed" to the Christian faith. Two out of three born-again believers assert that there is no such thing as absolute moral truth. There are other serious consequences as well:

First, millions of Christians view transformation in Christ as a onetime solution to a "crisis" rather than a lifelong "process." Many professing Christians presume that once a person has made peace with God by declaring Christ to be their eternal Protector, their spiritual journey has, for all intents and purposes, come to an end. Faith in God becomes a sort of spiritual "fire insurance policy" for when they die. The ceremonies, rituals, prayers, teaching, and sacraments of the Church are not perceived to have any practical value.

Second, and perhaps as a consequence, many believers stop growing in their faith. When evaluating their life, instead of measuring their performance against God's commands, the standard for comparison is "Did I do better than the next guy?"

Third, many Christians have developed a distorted understanding of what constitutes purposeful or successful living. When asked to describe the ends they live for, the top items most American Christians reported were good health, a successful career, a comfortable lifestyle, and a functional family. The average Christian assumes that when we are happy, God is happy.

Fourth, a large majority of Christians contend that the true meaning of our earthly existence is to simply enjoy life and reap as much fulfillment as we can from our daily pursuits. Even though most believers acknowledge that their blessings come from God, they further contend that the primary purpose of His blessings is to make them happy. Only a relative handful of believers are aware of God's explanation of the reasons for blessing us— namely, that we should become a blessing to others (see Gen. 12:1–3).

Finally, Christians are not prepared to fight the good fight of faith. We've lost sight of how the history of God's creation and people has unfolded, having become fully insulated within a culture that esteems achievement and comfort over sacrifice and suffering. We're not prepared to fight any fight at all; we look for God's hand of deliverance and blessing in the midst of hardships and challenges, rather than seek ways to serve others immersed in similar—or even more difficult—situations.

This lack of biblical literacy affects us not only individually but corporately. This is true on two levels. First, it affects church unity. When we claim to be followers of Christ but lack a biblical view of reality, the Church itself cannot be unified. Without a worldview shaped by the Bible, our efforts are, by default, shaped by the subjective and conflicting standards of other organizations, groups, and systems.

Second, our lack of biblical literacy is preventing us from reaching nonbelievers with the gospel message. To persuade a highly secularized and skeptical people that turning their life over to Christ is the only solution to emptiness and anomie, Christians must be credible. But how believable are we when the essence of our message must be "Do as I say, not as I do"? As long as American Christians model a faith based on complacency, convenience, and narcissism, living no differently from anyone else, our evangelistic witness will be hollow. Although in a desperate search for spiritual truth unbelievers may venture inside church doors, without a truly convincing reason to take God seriously non-Christians will not stay for long.

POISED FOR DEFEAT?

If we are ever going to witness the second coming of the Church, we must strengthen our spiritual muscles and gird ourselves with the truth of God's Word. Paul cautioned us to be prepared because we are involved in a fight to the finish, a spiritual battle that spans both the material and immaterial worlds.

> For our struggle is not against flesh and blood, but against the rulers,
> against the authorities, against the powers of this dark world and against
> the spiritual forces of evil in the heavenly realms.
>
> EPHESIANS 6:12

He used military metaphors to describe the spiritual warfare in which we are involved. In 1 Timothy 6:12, Paul instructed us to "fight the good fight of the faith." In Ephesians 6:13–18 he described the weapons at our disposal that will help us to win that fight.

Once we declare our side—good or evil, heaven or hell, Christ or Satan—then the battle rages on, around us and within us. Although we know that God and His true followers will be victorious in the end, that does not mean that there will not be many casualties along the route to victory.

It is a basic assumption of military strategy that if you hope to win, your troops must:

- be aware that a battle is coming;

- be psychologically and emotionally prepared to fight the battle; and

- be equipped with the resources to fight effectively.

Based on these three factors, most Christians are poised for an ignominious defeat. A majority of Christians do not take Satan seriously, and do not believe that there is any type of spiritual warfare taking place today. Most believers are so overwhelmed by the expectations of the world that they have lost touch with God's grand plan and His expectations for their life. Local churches have had little effect on the perspectives and pursuits of believers, rendering them defenseless in the contest for people's undivided allegiance.

Shortly before He was arrested, abused, and killed, Jesus prayed for His followers:

> I have given them your word and the world has hated them, for they are not of the world any more than I am of the world. My prayer is not that you take them out of the world but that you protect them from the evil one. They are not of the world, even as I am not of it. Sanctify them by the truth; your word is truth.
>
> JOHN 17:14–17

This is the well-known call for us, as disciples of Jesus, to be in the world but not of it, to be change agents for God. To fulfill that mandate, however, *we* must be changed first, and Jesus' prayer notes that the change comes from our wholehearted adoption of God's truth.

If we are serious about restoring the Church to vitality and serving as a cultural stimulant toward a moral and spiritual revolution, we must raise up a body of believers whose decisions in life are fully informed by their faith. For this to happen, we must help Christians develop a biblical worldview, and live in accordance with it.

[TEN]
A VISION FOR SPIRITUAL RENEWAL

LIFE IS A SERIES OF TRANSACTIONS. People invest in emotional, material, intellectual, physical, and spiritual transactions each day of their lives in order to satisfy basic needs and to fulfill their dreams. We are constantly on the lookout for opportunities to make life more meaningful, more pleasant, and more satisfying.

As change and innovations are introduced in every sphere of reality, the nature of our transactions changes. We reprioritize our activities, set different goals, develop new relationships, and reallocate our resources so that we may take advantage of emerging opportunities and alternatives.

In recent years, technological developments have sparked enormous changes in how we pursue our objectives. Technological advances, organizational restructuring, strategic alliances, marketplace decentralization, and consumer independence have redefined not only the players, but also the very character of the game. Organizations that used to dominate their respective industries, such as General Motors, RCA, Sears, and CBS, are struggling to maintain a toehold in the markets over which they used to reign. The factors that used to assure customer loyalty—reputation, location, size, familiarity, reliability, and even quality—no longer guarantee corporate success.

In fact, the changes occurring in our society are reshaping the transactions that define our existence. For example, banks used to believe that personal contact was a key to retaining customers and giving them a sense of the security of their money and the personal service of "their" banker. Financial transactions were forever redefined, however, with the introduction of the ATM.

The same magnitude of change is redefining the ministry domain. Several decades ago, the big focus was upon the decline of the mainline denominations. Mainline churches and their organizational superstructures lost touch with the people, triggering a massive outflow of adherents. The debate quickly shifted to issues of worship style (liturgical versus seeker-friendly) and ministry size (the bigger, the better, versus smallness brings intimacy).

Today the debate continues, but on a much more fundamental scale. Instead of choosing between one Protestant church or another, an increasing number of Americans are choosing between Christianity and other faith groups.

The search for the perfect "worship experience"—liturgical versus non-ritualistic, formal versus casual, traditional versus contemporary, active versus passive worship styles—has caused more and more people to opt for a mix of churches that will satiate their need for variety and depth of experience. The size of a church is no longer the issue; this consideration has been replaced by other, more pressing, concerns: relevance, relationships, and practical benefits.

So today the Church is at a crossroads. It must decide if it wishes to defend its traditional structure, as represented by the congregational format, for the delivery of ministry benefits and opportunities, or if it will reengineer itself in a way that allows it to conform to its biblical mandate and still respond to the practical needs of its members. This is an incredibly significant decision.

Most of our research suggests that the typical church is structured in ways that prevent it from effectively ministering to people. In most cases, the very organizational framework of the congregational church is inappropriate for addressing the needs resident in today's world. No matter how tenderhearted the people leading those churches may be, the design of the typical local church—which remains the primary model for the delivery of ministry—sets them (and us) up for defeat.

WE NEED TO START OVER

There was a time when the church on the corner was a central part of most people's lives, and those who participated in the life of the church were demonstrably better off for their investment of time and energy. Whenever the doors opened—several times each week—people would gather; a significant amount of the social life of the community centered around church activities.

People didn't move around as much then as they do now, and generations of families would band together to serve, support, and be supported by one another. The pastor was a respected figure in the community; from the pulpit he wielded a great deal of power. In its heyday, the congregational church was a respectable and reliable vehicle for delivering transformational ministry experiences. But its era is rapidly coming to a close.

Today the portrait is utterly different. Clergy have little influence in people's lives or in matters of cultural determination. Churches compete for people's attention and time, not only within the faith arena, but also with other economic, leisure, and community options. Basic concepts such as "absolute moral truth" have been trashed. Notions of loyalty to one God, one Savior, one Church, or even one theologically consistent belief system have been replaced by the perceptions that all faiths teach the same lessons, no faith is better than any other, there are no absolute faith principles, and religious truth can be customized to meet one's personal needs.

Although the times have changed, most churches have not; we often confuse structure and methods with theology and message. As a result, literally tens of thousands of churches are woefully out of synch with the people they most want to seek, save, serve, and send.

In Chapter 7 we discussed the six pillars of the unsinkable Church. Knowing the pillars on which we build the Church is necessary, but that knowledge, by itself, is not enough to facilitate the emergence of the true Church.

What Can We Learn from the Early Church?

There are a number of things about building the authentic church that we can learn both from Jesus' ministry and the activities of the early Church.

We know that Jesus seemed more intent on the quality of ministry than on the quantity of people He was able to touch. His primary investment was not in the crowds that flocked to see Him but in the core of leaders He lived with and mentored as the backbone of the first-century Church. He was most concerned with whether or not the apostles achieved a deep understanding of the Christian faith. He knew that if they really got it, they would be devoted to spreading it. A larger and growing quantity of believers would come as a result of quality in discipleship.

Second, Jesus showed His followers that the Church is truly different from existing pagan and religious groups only if Christians are known for the quality of their hearts. In other words, their reputation must be unlike that of any other group: They must be known as the most loving, most sincere, and most caring group of people around. This goes far deeper than mere friendliness. The Church that glorifies Jesus Christ ought to be known by the depth and consistency of its love of all people—especially love of other believers.

Third, a hallmark of the early Church was its integrity. This was realized through an intense commitment to accountability. If believers sinned and showed no signs of acknowledgment and repentance, they were confronted. If the church preached one view but collectively lived another, individuals would call the Church to repent. Paul's letters to the church in Corinth are examples of how seriously the early Church guarded the quality of believers' lives. And the experience in Acts 6 where the Church was accused of abandoning the needs of its widows is yet another sign of its devotion to integrity.

Fourth, the first-century Church was distinguished by its attitude. Specifically, the Christians of the day felt a sense of urgency about ministry. Not knowing when Christ would return, and acutely aware that the ministry agenda He had outlined was of the utmost significance, they felt a need to be diligent about ministry. They also exhibited an intense passion for Christ and for serving Him with their lives. And they were committed to doing their service with excellence because they knew it reflected their own depth of commitment to Christ.

Fifth, the Lord would have searched for evidence of dependence on God. Constant and wholehearted engagement in worship suggests our recognition of our own insignificance and an understanding of the awesomeness of God. Investing substantial time and energy in prayer is another indication of our reliance upon God. Even the degree to which we count on the Church as a central means of emotional and spiritual support is a signal of our devotion to the resources provided by God for our strength and development.

Finally, the true Church is strategic in its response to conditions and opportunities. We cannot be so enamored of our ministry plans and traditions that we ignore reality. When conditions change, the Church's responses must also change. Operating in ways that fulfill God's vision for our lives and ministries requires that we hold the vision constant but the plans and strategies as flexible guides toward our vision-based goals. Jesus' ministry was a study in challenging assumptions; addressing unforeseen windows of opportunity; and modifying expectations in light of the bigger picture of ministry outcomes.

THREE STRATEGIC THRUSTS

Given what we have learned about our culture, the Church in America, and how we can create a strategic response to challenging conditions, I am convinced that the Church must pursue a three-pronged strategy for renewal. The aggressive and intelligent pursuit of these three outcomes will position the Church for strength and impact for years to come, enabling Christianity to successfully compete for the minds, hearts, and souls of the people.

First, we must motivate people to pursue, embrace, and live according to a biblical worldview. Churches today are filled with people who claim they are Christians but who demonstrate no depth of understanding or consistent application of core biblical principles. Before believers act like Christians they must learn to think like Christians.

Indeed, if we are to influence our culture, non-Christians must be attracted to the difference that being Christian makes in the lives of its adherents. In our highly competitive culture, Christians must stand out because of the positive influence their faith has upon their lives. Millions of Christians desire to live in such a manner; millions more would desire such a lifestyle if they could see what it looked like and thus realize what is missing in their own spiritual development.

Second, we must allow the Church to be led by the people whom God has called and anointed for that task—that is, leaders. As long as the Church persists in being led by teachers, it will flounder. Identifying, developing, deploying, and supporting gifted leaders will renew the vision, energy, and impact of the Church.

Most of the leaders that need to be invited and nurtured within ministeries will be laypeople. While seminaries may produce some of our future leaders, the majority will arise from within our congregations to sharpen their leadership abilities and use the leadership gifts they possess.

Third, we must develop new forums and formats through which people will experience, understand, and serve God. New models of the Church must be allowed to blossom—models that reflect the diversity of needs, opportunities, and perspectives that define our culture. These new models will make the Christian faith accessible and relevant to people who otherwise would not consider Christianity to be an option worthy of exploration.

In the chapters to come, let's examine what we might do to facilitate the second coming of the Church.

[ELEVEN]
CULTIVATING A BIBLICAL WORLDVIEW

GETTING PEOPLE TO UNDERSTAND the importance of a biblical world-view and to pursue it may be more difficult than you think. Most Americans do not have an intentionally developed worldview, but they have become comfortable with the way things are. Even the relatively small number of people who have what they consider to be a worldview may not be open to reevaluating their perspective.

Roughly one-quarter of all American adults claim that their worldview is inherently founded on biblical principles. And yet, when asked to describe the content of that worldview, or to explain how they arrived at their understanding of truth, meaning, and appropriate behavior, less than one in ten were able to do so.[1] The research suggests that most people's worldview is little more than a collection of fragmented ideals mindlessly adopted from pop culture.

Unfortunately, few Christians are currently involved in the disciplines necessary to integrate scriptural truth in daily life. Our most recent surveys indicate that about half of all adults listen to preaching or Bible teaching in a typical week; one out of three read the Bible; one out of ten study the Bible during the week; and fewer than one out of every twenty-five devote themselves to memorizing at least one new Bible verse during a typical week. Less than 2 percent are committed to all four of these practices on a weekly basis. It's no wonder Americans have tremendous spiritual hunger, but no consistent spiritual growth.

As disappointing as the reality may be, there are ways through which we may reverse this trend of moving away from biblical knowledge and application. Many years ago The Navigators, a disciple-making ministry located in Colorado, initiated a dynamic spiritual development process that gave

Christians a way to integrate the truths contained in Scripture into their daily lives. The process consists of five activities:

1. hearing the Word of God;

2. reading the Bible;

3. personal Bible study;

4. Bible memorization; and

5. meditating on the content of God's Word.[2]

If followed routinely and seriously, these five practices will lead to personal transformation and enable individuals to cultivate a worldview that is soundly grounded in scriptural principles.

Read the Bible

Reading straight through the Bible, from Genesis to Revelation, is the natural tendency of millions, but it may also be the most difficult way to make meaningful progress. In a recent study we discovered that only one out of every seven adults who read the Bible does so with a specific reading plan in mind. We also learned that the individuals who reflect spiritual maturity and commitment are those who have a regular and frequent time set aside for reading the Bible, and have some type of plan or topical focus to direct their selection of Bible passages to read.

Memorize Key Bible Verses

People most often profit from memorization when they relate the verses they are committing to memory to a topic or perspective of critical interest to them at the moment. Many individuals promote memorization as a means of fending off temptations during moments of vulnerability.

However, in terms of biblical worldview development, perhaps the greatest value of verse recall is the ability to memorize a "critical mass" of scriptural principles that will enable the believer to make good immediate judgments and decisions. Often, we do not have the luxury of time to look up passages and to reflect on their interrelation. Having those insights firmly in mind expedites the process of thinking and behaving "Christianly."

Listen to Targeted Teaching

This includes sermons, lessons, and tapes on topics related to an aspect of a Christian worldview. Often, we hear sermons and teaching that are biblically sound and well presented, but of little practical value or particular use in developing a Christian mind.

Imagine you have been asked to prepare a report on the character of God. Based on your belief that God created everything you conclude that knowing as much as you can about every topic will allow you to discover elements of God's character. So you go to the library and start reading every book there, searching for insights into God's character. Along the way, of course, you gain exposure to aspects of His character as well as numerous other fascinating and potentially useful tidbits of information. However, before long you realize a couple of things. First, you'll never finish the task—there is just too much to absorb. Second, without a more definitive framework of analysis, you will be overwhelmed with information and will probably not arrive at insightful conclusions.

Similarly, if we're trying to get the big picture of God, humanity, and life, listening to a random selection of biblical teachings won't hurt, but it probably won't help much, either. Identifying the topics you need to learn, then intentionally pursuing information, understanding, and applications regarding those topic is a more appropriate approach.

Study the Bible

There are various ways of gleaning truths and principles from the Bible. The method of study may not be as crucial to your development as your commitment to such study, and the topics or passages chosen for in-depth research and reflection.

Rather than collecting numerous facts from the Bible, your ultimate goal should be to create a comprehensive, Scripture-based perspective that impacts how you understand and relate to the world around you. Enter your study with a particular question or focus and search out passages that illuminate your thinking. Use reference books such as concordances, commentaries, and Bible dictionaries to clarify what you are reading. Allow the Bible to provide the contextual interpretation so that you do not introduce indefensible or inaccurate biases into your study.

Read Developmental Books

There are thousands of books written about the content of the Bible and Christian living. Selecting those that focus on topics and issues directly relevant to your quest for a biblical worldview can be invaluable. Having discussions with one or two others who read the same materials can deepen your commitment to the process, your comprehension of key points, and your retention of valuable concepts.

While such reading should never substitute for reading the Bible itself, absorbing these publications can be a worthwhile supplement to Scripture reading.

Meditate

Take time to reflect on what you are hearing, reading, seeing, feeling, and experiencing. One of the great tragedies of American life is that we are so wrapped up in having as many experiences as possible, we rarely stop to think about what we have undergone and what it all means.

To develop a biblical worldview, you absolutely must take time on a regular basis to reflect. If your schedule seems too packed to fit in think time, try this: Cut the amount of time you're devoting to reading, listening, observing, or experiencing, and devote the time saved to reflecting on what you were exposed to. That practice alone will heighten your retention and comprehension substantially.

Discuss Your Insights and Questions

Few people learn best in total isolation; even those who prefer a measure of solitude can greatly benefit from others who are also on a quest for a biblical worldview.

Most people learn better through interactive processes. Varying the form of interaction and your interactive partners may further enhance what you glean.

Try role-playing. Try holding a Socratic conversation, in which you state and restate your position and ask your peer questions about his or her position. Get on the Internet and correspond with others—in a chat room or via E-mail—who share an interest in your current topic of exploration. Convene a small group that will meet regularly to discuss predetermined issues and matters associated with your mutual quest for a biblical worldview.

Get a Good Coach

Identify a mature Christian, one who possesses a biblical worldview, and ask that person to be a personal coach or mentor to you. You might ask your pastor or other spiritual person for recommendations if he or she does not have time to commit to that role themselves.

When you are evaluating the suitability of a particular mentor, look for the following attributes in that person:

- possesses obvious spiritual maturity, humility, and wisdom;
- is willing to commit to spending time with you;
- possesses spiritual gifts that are consistent with your needs: a gifted teacher, counselor, shepherd, exhorter, or pastor;
- can be "transparent" with you, is willing to be vulnerable;
- possesses a high level of integrity;
- views the relationship as an opportunity for mutual growth;
- possesses a servant orientation; and
- "connects" with you on a personal level, based on common experiences, background, or vision.

Once you have selected your mentor, establish a regular meeting time to discuss the areas of your spiritual life that need to develop, and for which you need accountability. Ask that person to recommend materials for your personal study, and discuss them with your mentor.

When possible, it is also good to get to know your mentor more informally. Hang out with that person in public and with your families; how does his or her worldview influence the way he or she behaves? Does his or her behavior differ from your own inclinations? If so, are the differences due to personal style or spiritual principles?

THE ROLE OF THE CHURCH

While it is true that each individual is ultimately responsible for ensuring that his or her own worldview is in agreement with scriptural truth, there are a number of things the Church can and must do to help with this process. One of the most important things we can do is to *motivate people to desire a biblical worldview.* This can happen any number of ways. We can model this behavior ourselves; people mimic the actions they observe of their respected peers. We can saturate our church ministries with a worldview mentality, creating new ministries designed to promote a biblical worldview, or adapt existing ministries as needed. Finally, we can motivate the desire for a biblical worldview among our congregations through the ministry visions cast by church leaders. People respond to the confident vision and wisdom of godly leadership.

In addition to creating a desire for a biblical worldview among its members, the Church must also *be a resource to growing Christians.* The kinds of resources provided—and needed—will vary from believer to believer and from church to church. However, if a church is serious about investing in the spiritual development of its people, it may seek to provide five basic resources to its people:

- *Assistance in charting a plan to develop a biblical worldview.* There are certain kinds of tools every Christian needs in order to cultivate a biblical worldview. The church must help its members to understand what resources are available—and how to use them. Ultimately,the church may wish to assist the believer in forming an agenda for growth.

- *Biblically based instruction that will challenge and inform believers.* The role of instructing Christians in the content of the Bible, and how to interpret its content in light of everyday experiences, is appropriate and worthwhile.

- *Materials that will aid each person's development.* There is no vacuum of materials available about the Christian faith and the content of the Bible. The church might serve as a clearinghouse for materials, providing counsel as to which materials would be most valuable to an individual given their agenda for growth and the stage they are at on that agenda.

- *Personal counseling to facilitate individual growth.* One of the most significant contributions a church can make to any believer's growth process is the coaching provided by a Christian who has already developed a biblical worldview.

- *A means of holding individuals accountable.* Spiritually mature teachers, leaders, and mentors make an important contribution in the lives of others when they hold those they counsel accountable for their own behavior. By helping new believers to evaluate their current behavior, to define specific problem areas, and to establish a plan for change, spiritually mature Christians can assist in the growth process of other believers.

Create a "Discomfort Zone"

We often learn best and think most clearly when we are forced to do so. One way to hone your biblical worldview is to develop true friendships with people who are intelligent, reflective non-Christians, and to engage those individuals in respectful, consistent dialogue about their values and ideas. Some Christians think such relationships are useful primarily for evangelistic purposes, but many others have found the challenge provided by such conversations to be incredibly powerful personal growth stimulants.

There are other ways to dismantle that comfortable learning (or vegetating) cocoon as well. Visit events sponsored by other faith groups to better understand competing points of view. (This would be in addition to, not in place of, your time commitment to your regular church.)

Once you have progressed enough to do so, you might assume responsibility to teach young people about an integrated Christian faith. The challenge of facing head-on their honest questions can hone your own wisdom; however, you will want to be sufficiently grounded in your own faith so that you won't hinder someone else's spiritual growth! If you prefer to write rather than teach, try submitting a paper containing the framework of your biblical worldview to professors or other trusted Christian thinkers who will constructively critique your assessment.

The essence of all of these endeavors, of course, is to evaluate your growth or to propel it by taking relatively safe but challenging risks.

Act on It

As you develop your biblical worldview, it should affect your behavior. To test your depth and clarity, identify a political issue, a personal financial challenge, a relationship, or some other event or condition that's important in your life.

Once you have identified this event or condition, set a course of action based upon the precepts of your emerging worldview. For example, if you have overextended yourself with revolving debt, as you read about scriptural principles of handling money you might become aware that your current situation does not glorify God. After asking Him for forgiveness and praying for wisdom, determine what you need to do to get yourself out of debt. If you have a broken relationship within your family, you might study what the Bible has to say about forgiveness and reconciliation, then map a plan of action to restore the relationship.

Once you have mapped out a course of action, follow that reasoning to its logical conclusion and engage others affected by your decision. Does your wife agree with your financial assessment? Are there others in your family who have been affected by this broken relationship and who could give you advice on how to best mend the breech?

The challenges associated with experiments like these should strengthen your character, sharpen your mind, clarify your values and beliefs, and prepare you to think "Christianly." It is a process that takes time, forces numerous mistakes, and is sometimes fulfilling and often uncomfortable. However, the end result is that you will gradually become the mature person of Christ that you have been called to become.

Remember that we have not been called to be comfortable, but obedient. Developing the mind of Christ is a forerunner to exhibiting the lifestyle of Christ, which reflects obedience to God.

WHAT ARE THE SPECIFIC PRINCIPLES
OF A "BIBLICAL WORLDVIEW"?

The information woven into your worldview is of the utmost importance, since it will shape your notion of who God is, who you are, your relationship to God and His world, and your purposes and parameters in life.

I don't want to discourage you, but please realize that you will never possess a perfect Christian worldview, no matter how hard you try and how long you pursue it. As human beings, we have two main hindrances:

- *First, we are mortal.* There is simply too much to know, and too little time to learn it. Scripture is saturated with truth that we must gradually integrate, with the help of the Holy Spirit. Even so, our human limitations prevent us from completely and perfectly absorbing and applying all biblical truth.

- *Second, we are not omniscient.* This side of heaven, we continue to have only an imperfect understanding of many spiritual truths. No matter how much we study, much will always remain hidden from us.

These limitations aside, you should bear in mind that no one can impose the content of a meaningful biblical worldview upon you. While the objective standard of Scripture clearly teaches right from wrong, how we apply these principles to our lives depends upon a number of other factors.

We all think and learn differently. We have vastly divergent experiences and abilities. Consequently, the approach we use and the information we integrate will necessarily differ. We may wind up with roughly equivalent perspectives, but how we arrive at the similar outcomes, and how we synthesize them into our lives will reflect our unique personalities, intelligence, sensitivities, and vision.

But perhaps I can offer some guiding thoughts in relation to determining the content of your worldview. Let me offer two distinct approaches to developing your worldview. First, you might consider the topics that would be most helpful in defining your worldview. Second, we might reflect on key Scripture passages that will help you develop that worldview.

IDENTIFY THE TOPICS
INCLUDED IN YOUR BIBLICAL WORLDVIEW

Since the idea of a worldview is that it provides a mental filter that influences all of your thoughts and actions, virtually every topic could somehow be related to the development of your grand perspective on life, truth, and meaning. However, we must identify the basics in the beginning, then expand from there to develop a more comprehensive, working worldview. Where would you start?

One process that people have used is to identify topics that address the core issues of life, especially those topics with which you have constant interaction. You may distill such a list by considering the key public issues of the day, common topics of discussion you have among peers, and significant decisions relevant to your life. Here are examples of topics you may choose to incorporate into such a process:

- salvation, grace, sin, and forgiveness
- conquering the power of sin
- the significance of Christian fellowship
- the lordship of Jesus Christ
- the content and implications of faith
- the understanding, experiencing, and giving of love
- stewardship of resources
- the will of God and the will of humans
- obedience to God
- the roles and influence of the Trinity
- the reality and influence of Satan
- the return of Jesus Christ
- compassion, generosity, and service
- global vision
- the Christian's responsibility to government

- social policy regarding homosexuality, divorce, euthanasia, abortion, and the death penalty
- ethics in business
- practical morality[3]

One leading advocate of Christian thinking has proposed a different set of topics. Harry Blamires, a student of C. S. Lewis, talks about scrutinizing the Bible to derive a worldview that addresses:

- our orientation to the supernatural
- an awareness of good and evil
- acceptance of authority
- concern for other people and
- our conception of truth.[4]

While somewhat more esoteric or scholarly in approach, incisive reflection on such matters could certainly produce a coherent line of reasoning that would serve a believer well.

Realize, of course, that your unique frame of reference, thinking style, and experience base will cause you to draw upon a different set of topics. That's fine, as long as the topics you select enable you to arrive at a true biblical worldview.

Draw from Scripture to Identify the Basics

An alternative approach is to identify key Scripture verses that have endowed your faith with both depth and breadth. This tactic presupposes that you have a rather comprehensive familiarity with Scripture and that you have already developed a mental model of what is most important to draw from the Bible as fundamental truths for your worldview.

Of course, those who do not have such a comprehensive familiarity with Scripture will not gravitate to this approach. However, this approach need not be intimidating: Every means to developing a worldview is based on a model of significant traits; those we initially select from the Word of God represent merely a starting point in a lifelong process of evolving a godly perspective on reality.

My developmental process has been a hybrid of both methods. In addition to studying about and reflecting on issue-oriented topics, my ruminations have been greatly advanced by focusing upon Bible passages that the Holy Spirit has impressed upon me. For instance, here is the list of passages that helped launch my effort to arrive at a biblical worldview.

- *Creation account and the Fall (Gen. 1–3)*—Insight into God's power, plan, and provision, and humankind's weakness and dependence

- *The purpose of God's blessings (Gen. 12:1–3)*

- *The Ten Commandments (Ex. 20:1–16)*—God's expectations of me

- *The purpose of my life (Deut. 6:5)*

- *The significance of God's vision for my life (Prov. 29:18)*

- *What really matters in life (Eccl. 12:13–14)*

- *A prophetic view of the coming and purpose of Jesus Christ (Isa. 53)*

- *An addendum to what God expects of me (Mic. 6:8)*

- *The Sermon on the Mount (Matt. 5–7)*—Fundamental principles of Christianity

- *Principles of disagreement and reconciliation (Matt. 18:15–18)*

- *A perspective on leadership and servanthood (Matt. 20:20–28)*

- *The most important commandments to God (Matt. 22:34–40)*

- *The Great Commission (Matt. 28:19)*—A reminder that my faith is to be shared, not hoarded

- *We are to live in this world but not sell out to it (John 17:14–19)*

- *A portrait of the authentic Church in action (Acts 2)*

- *Salvation, the indwelling Spirit, and perseverance (Rom. 8)*

- *Submission and authority (Rom. 13:1–7)*

- *Discipline within the Church, judgment beyond it (1 Cor. 5:9–6:11)*

- *Contextualizing ministry (1 Cor. 9:19–23)*
- *Understanding and utilizing spiritual gifts (1 Cor. 12)*
- *The potential for persecution, importance of passion (2 Cor. 11:22–33)*
- *Works of the flesh, fruit of the Spirit (Gal. 5:17–25)*
- *Family life (Eph. 5:22–6:4)*
- *The existence and nature of spiritual warfare (Eph. 6:10–20)*
- *Exhortations for holy living (1 Thess. 5:15–22)*
- *Qualifications of spiritual leaders (1 Tim. 3)*
- *The nature of faith (Heb. 11)*
- *Balance between faith and deeds (James 1:21–27; 2:14–18)*

This approach is not without flaws; if inappropriately developed, this approach could result in exactly the same type of hodgepodge of disconnected scriptural facts that has undermined the body of believers in recent years.

It also represents a significant departure from the "systematic theology" strategy that many seminaries teach.

And I suppose if we could arrange for all ninety million Christians in the United States to get appropriate schooling in systematic theology, the Church might be better off. The mix-and-match biblical potpourri I described above is far from perfect and potentially harmful.

But let's get real for a moment. How many of your friends are going to complete a theology program at a seminary? Not many. And how many churches offer a truly comprehensive and systematic survey of the Bible? Again, not many. In the meantime, then, we are better off instigating a perpetual self-driven discovery process than waiting for formal education procedures to influence the mass of believers.

The process is decidedly incremental, and it demands a long-term commitment to expanding the elements integrated into the resulting worldview. However, we must take the time required if we are going to establish a biblical worldview. There is no time like the present.

Time is short for the American church. We must immediately impress upon people's minds and hearts that having a biblical worldview is necessary;

it is not an optional pursuit. Perhaps you may earn the privilege of living in God's presence forever on the basis of a confession of faith. But the ability to make that faith tangible and meaningful *in this lifetime* demands that you have a transformed mind.

Let me offer a final word of encouragement. Perhaps the entire enterprise I am suggesting—namely, getting all believers to truly understand, embrace, and live according to Christian principles, values, and beliefs—seems like too huge an undertaking to even consider. I will admit, it is a massive undertaking.

However, it is very doable. Play the numbers game with me for a moment. We have somewhere in the neighborhood of eighty million adult believers in the United States. Since perhaps 10 percent currently possess a biblical worldview, they become our foundation upon which we will build. Let's imagine that each of those individuals took on just three people to coach in worldview development over the course of the next two years. After twenty-four months, we'd jump from 10 percent to 40 percent of the Christian population possessing a biblical worldview. Repeat the process, using that 40 percent as the new base of coaches. Let's lighten the load and say each worldview Christian took two believers under his or her wing. There would not even be enough worldview-starved believers to team with all of the coaches available. Most important within four years we could theoretically wipe out biblical illiteracy and indifference among the body of Christ.

Back to reality. I am fully aware that we would never get all 10 percent of the existing foundation of worldview Christians to engage in a coaching relationship with three worldview-lacking Christians. And I realize that for some believers, two years would not be a long enough period of time to acquire even a fundamental worldview condition. The point, however, is not that we would fail to help transform the minds and lives of every Christian, but that we can make very serious inroads into the spiritual superficiality of the Church in less than five years—if we're really committed to this goal.

How committed are you?

[TWELVE]
HOW TO TRAIN NEW LEADERS

IN CHAPTER EIGHT WE DEFINED the three characteristics of Christian leaders as well as the four types of leaders each church needs at various stages of its ministry. Now that we know what we're looking for, and have established that the majority of pastors serving in churches today do not have the gift of leadership, then where are the real leaders?

Fortunately, we don't have to look any farther than the next pew. The natural solution to enhancing both the quality and the quantity of leadership within any church is to empower laypeople to use their leadership gifts in various churchwide capacities.

Why aren't there more laity presently involved in leading God's people forward? In discussing this with a wide range of Christians whose leadership abilities were clearly visible outside the Church realm, several reasons were commonly raised when asked why they were not using their gifts *inside* the Church:

- They had never been invited to lead;
- they don't have time; and
- they don't want to use their talents in the Church.

But why would Christians with leadership gifts not want to use them in the Church? Based on our extensive work with churches, we might add what may be the most common reason of all:

Many pastors, feeling threatened by the presence and abilities of true leaders, consequently make it impossible or uncomfortable for laity to lead.

Leaders are among the busiest people in our society. Because their talent is needed in every organization and enhances the activities of every group, leaders are typically spread thin. Adding church duties to their roster of responsibilities is not compelling—especially when the person in the position of senior leadership is not excited about enlisting their services.

A number of lay Christians also noted that their experience has shown that leading in the Church does not bring the same level of satisfaction or fulfillment as leading in the "real world" because of the limitations of church life. The most common limitations included the lack of resources to do ministry properly, restrictive organizational structures and requirements, and the unlikely prospects of being able to develop a team with a sense of vision cohesive enough to make significant progress.

When true leaders find themselves in situations in which they are forced to submit to the leadership of someone who does not have leadership capabilities, one of two options usually results: Either they accept the situation and wait patiently for an opportunity to serve, or they quit. Since the middle of 1995, our data have shown a consistent flight of lay leaders from the Church, largely because they are appalled by the inferior existing leadership, and frustrated by the inability to contribute their leadership know-how to the Church. This is a trend that the Church overlooks at its own peril. We must find, train, and unleash those to whom God has given leadership abilities—and we must do it quickly.

LEADERSHIP TRAINING: THE LIFEBLOOD OF THE FUTURE CHURCH

Helping leaders develop their gifts is no simple task. While two of the identifying traits of leaders—calling and character—may need to be reinforced, competencies must be gradually instilled within these potential leaders.

When it comes to developing the competencies of leaders, we must also bear in mind that we are working with people who will be leading at different levels of responsibility (micro, mezzo, macro); who possess different leadership aptitudes (Directing, Team-Building, Strategic, Operational); and who will ebb and flow with the changing tide of the ministry's culture (through periods of Infancy, Development, Maturity, and Decline).

In spite of this multilayered complexity, the evidence indicates that a well-designed training approach can enhance the leadership competencies of those who have been called to the task of leading God's people.

Whom Should We Develop?

On the one hand, we know that virtually every Christian is called to exhibit leadership in some dimensions of life, operating on the microlevel. The family is a great example of this need. Fathers are called to be the spiritual leaders of their families, mothers are called to be moral and family leaders to their children, and even older children are responsible to lead their younger siblings to appropriate maturity.

There are times when each of us, regardless of our position or background, is relied upon to provide situational leadership—on the job, in a classroom, during a moment of crisis, or in other fluid moments of life. Every Christian needs to know basic leadership principles and to strive to achieve the essential qualities of a Christian leader.

On the other hand, the type of leadership development that is most sorely lacking is that which identifies and nurtures people who will provide intentional leadership in areas beyond the bare necessities required for survival. This runs the gamut from people leading a small group that meets in someone's home twice a month for a time of Bible study and prayer to global evangelists and Christian statesmen.

Qualities of Future Leaders

All Christians—whether they are primarily providing family, situational, or extended intentional leadership—need to learn the basic characteristics of godly leadership. At the very least, understanding what makes a person a good leader will enhance our ability to be responsible followers toward seeing the kingdom of God develop. Developing leadership qualities and abilities into our lives can only draw us nearer to God and prepare us for ever more exciting opportunities to be used by Him.

However, there are millions of believers who are providing extended, intentional leadership who need more extensive training in the art of leading people. Discerning who these people are is one of the challenges facing current church leaders. Here are a few of the qualities to seek in trying to identify the influential leaders of the future.

They have led people in the past. Individuals with an inclination to lead cannot deny or diminish that inclination. Look for evidence of previous involvement in leading people.

They resonate with vision. Every leader must initiate or advance God's vision for a group of people. If they are unable either to see or to support a sense of purpose beyond the group's immediate circumstances, then chances are good they have not been called to lead on an extended level.

They are anxious to create meaningful change. Leaders realize that progress only results from improving existing realities. People who support the status quo may be gifted managers, but they are not leaders. Leaders are willing to shatter the comfort zone and initiate new and better ways of doing things.

They are responsible. Leaders are not flakes. They can be counted on by other people to conceive realistic ideas, promote planned change, and follow through on their ideas, their promises, and their mistakes. Unless a person can be counted on to do what is best for others, he or she is not a leader.

They have courage. Many of the core tasks of leading people—resolving conflict, championing change, mobilizing volunteer servants, evaluating performance—demand a level of resilience and fortitude. Wimps may be lovable, but they are not reliable as leaders.

Courage based on the conviction of calling, confidence in competencies, and faith in God's wisdom and love is an insurmountable attribute in a leader. If they consistently exude honesty, speaking the truth in love, and make the tough calls when no one else wants to, they have courage.

They love God. Christian leaders are distinct from worldly leaders in that:

- Their primary *focus* is God's vision;
- their primary *commitment* is serving God; and
- their primary *goal* is obedience to Him.

A mark of a Christian leader is that his or her focus is not upon personal accomplishment but upon doing that which brings glory, honor, and pleasure to God.

They learn quickly and continually. Leaders are learners. Great leaders are always seeking new insights so they can fine-tune their understanding of the future and the opportunities it brings.

If someone deliberately seeks new information and experiences that will upgrade his or her ability to understand things and to help people, chances are good that the person is a leader.[1]

Training Principles

Most ministries have limited resources to invest in training leaders. Use your resources wisely by investing in the people with the highest potential to influence the Church. Let's assume that you have read the signs and have identified individuals with high leadership potential. What do you do to develop their potential?

The appropriate approach will vary from individual to individual. For example, many of those who have been targeted for Christian leadership have impressive track records of effective leadership in the business world, or in other community endeavors. The Church needs to assist these people to supplement their existing skills with additional abilities that will help them use their "secular" skills in a Christian environment. Often, these people need to focus on character development to strengthen personal attributes that are not promoted in the workplace but are essential to Christian-oriented leadership.

Other potential Christian leaders may be younger adults who are still probing their own capabilities and interests and are just discovering their enjoyment and impact in leading others. How can you develop all of these individuals into the leadership champions God intended?

No matter how you proceed, there are some universal principles that will help you to train your leaders more appropriately. Consider how you might incorporate these principles into the leadership development process with which you are involved.

PRINCIPLE #1:
Personalize the Process

Just as there is no single style of ministry that satisfies everyone, neither is there a single leadership development curriculum, program, or approach that will perfectly fit every growing Christian leader.

The most effective processes I have studied are those that have been customized to address the specific needs and idiosyncrasies of the individual in training. Research conducted by professional training companies has demonstrated that the more personalized the developmental process, the more lasting and life-changing the impact.

Create "growth partners." A key to personalizing the development process effectively is to incorporate "growth partners." These are individuals who serve as "personal trainers" to the nascent leader. In the same way that a master electrician would train an apprentice, the master leader seeks to foster the consistent growth of his or her junior peer.

For instance, in areas of leadership where the emerging leader has refined skills, the growth partner may provide encouragement. In dimensions of leadership where the emerging leader is a neophyte and needs substantial help, the growth partner may follow the hallowed training pattern:

- *I do, you watch;*
- *I do, you assist;*
- *You do, I assist;*
- *You do, I watch;*
- *You do it alone.*

In every situation, the training provided is geared to the unique needs of the emerging leader. For individuals who have been called by God to lead but have little or no prior leadership experience, such training will address both character and competency issues.

Other benefits of the mentor relationship. This mentoring process can be adapted by the master leader or mentor to impart any number of personal growth goals for the aspiring leader. The context of this relationship provides other benefits as well: accountability in matters related to character; sincere encouragement and honest feedback as the aspiring leader acquires new competencies; and a way to model different types of leadership behaviors and skills.

The value of personalization cannot be overestimated. People lose interest and their growth curve plateaus when they are subjected to generic training. When a respected leader invests personal time in them, though, the message sent is "I'm important and my development as a leader must really matter to the Church."

PRINCIPLE #2:
Development Is a Continual Process

Leadership development is never an event or a destination. As growth occurs, emerging leaders will reach certain destination points along the journey, but nobody has ever completely mastered the art of leading people. There is always more to learn, new experiences to have, new ideas to consider, new strategies to try.

Many of the more successful ministries have learned that developing leaders is a lifelong challenge, requiring different levels of training accessible at all times. The most effective training processes are those which gradually heighten the intensity of the leadership applications. Once individuals prove themselves in tasks of minor impact, promote them to more challenging tasks, allowing them to rise to their personal ceiling. Once that point has been reached, the focus of the training may shift to broadening, rather than deepening, their impact.

PRINCIPLE #3:
The Emerging Leader Should Push the Process

In the past, many ministries have taken full responsibility for the training of potential leaders. However, just as Christians are to be responsible for their own spiritual growth, so emerging leaders must help to set the pace for developing their leadership competencies.

A ministry may rightfully insist upon potential leaders investing themselves in leadership development activities. However, it is the emerging leader—not the group providing the leadership opportunities— who should initiate and spearhead the equipping process. This is perhaps the first step a potential leader may take toward signifying a call to and passion for transformational leadership.

Consider the wisdom of having leaders help design and monitor their own development program. In a rapidly changing culture, the typical ministry, as an organization, is unlikely to provide a leading-edge, evolving process for meeting the developmental needs of its new leaders.

Further, the people we are describing as "called and gifted to lead" already possess an innate ability to lead. What they lack are opportunities to apply their gifts and chances to reflect on the quality of their leadership with a competent and trustworthy leader who will give realistic feedback and useful guidance. Ultimately, a self-directed process makes the most sense if we conceptualize the leadership developers as facilitators of God-given abilities, rather than omniscient experts whose wisdom will radically redefine the very nature of the emerging leader.

The role of a master leader or mentor in the process is to ensure that the emerging leader undertakes a holistic program of development. Either through self-deception, lack of self-awareness, or a desire to avoid high-stress or high-anxiety challenges, some leaders-in-training overlook performance areas that need refinement. A master teacher can sharpen the emerging leader by calling attention to such oversights.

PRINCIPLE #4:
Maximize Leader Growth by
Creating a Positive Learning Environment

The conditions under which people are prepared for leadership influence their ability to reach their full potential. The ideal scenario is to create conditions in which learning can be maximized.

In addition to self-directed learning, here are a few additional ways in which learning, rather than mere exposure to instruction, enhances the development process.

Accept mistakes. Expecting perfection of someone who is learning a new art is unrealistic. When people believe they are penalized in some way for making mistakes, they take fewer risks and consequently they do not stretch themselves. Mistakes are a part of learning. Let emerging leaders know that their goal is growth and servanthood, not perfection.

Allow time for the lessons to "soak in." Learning takes time. Rushing people through a crash course in leadership is an exercise in futility. Many of the tasks leaders perform take some getting used to; others are counter-intuitive and thus require substantial time to own. Factual knowledge can be gained quickly; the heart of a leader changes slowly.

Vary the approaches used in training. Nothing becomes more tedious than the same approach used over and over, time after time. Incorporate different people, different instructional styles, divergent settings, a variety of media, case studies, varying levels of participation, and unexpected structures. Real-time leadership is a study in dealing with the unexpected. Equipping leaders through the use of an array of means will better prepare them for the challenges to come.

Balance the head and the heart. Some leaders learn most easily through emotional experiences, others grow most easily in response to intellectual efforts. However, research confirms that everyone learns best when an intellectual insight is fortified by an emotional experience. This wedding of head and heart, through the tandem of learning about and then doing, results in an unforgettable lesson that the person owns.

PRINCIPLE #5:

Specify the Importance of a

Biblical Worldview Before the Training Begins

Leadership always fits within a larger framework of life. To help shape a leader's abilities, it is important to examine her view of reality; her belief system serves as her filter on circumstances and has an impact on her decisions.

Emerging leaders should have an opportunity to closely examine their worldview early in the leadership development process. Dissecting values, assumptions, beliefs, and philosophies will provide significant insights into the character of the potential leader, and raise some important opportunities and obstacles related to leadership.

PRINCIPLE #6:
Intentionally Escalate the Prospects of Success

The overall purpose of leadership development is to prepare a person to lead with greater impact. The development process, then, is all about enabling the leader to be a superior change agent. You can facilitate small steps toward leadership maturity by doing things that set up the emerging leader for success. Examples of this include:

- Increasing the levels of responsibility assigned to the emerging leader;
- delegating the required levels of authority in decision-making situations;
- giving credit publicly for the good choices and efforts made by the emerging leader;
- treating failures not as setbacks but as an unexpected and effective lessons.

In working with up-and-coming leaders, we prepare them to assume increasing responsibility and to handle it adeptly. We can serve them best by gradually increasing the intensity of their challenges.

PRINCIPLE #7:
Pace the Process Appropriately

Often we overwhelm leaders with information and techniques and expect them to grasp everything at once. Leaders, even the most capable individuals, are only human. They learn most effectively when they are allowed to integrate one or two significant ideas at a time.

Leaders are, by nature, learners; they have a great capacity and thirst for learning. However, proper pacing is critical.

PRINCIPLE #8:
Never Underestimate the Power of Positive Reinforcement

If you want to ensure that an emerging leader picks up a particular idea or behavior, reinforce it. Adults are no different from children when it comes to personal growth habits: We disdain that which is painful, loathe making sacrifices, entertain and integrate only a few new concepts at a time, and embrace those concepts or responses that we find rewarding. Celebrate those responses that indicate the leader is growing.

PRINCIPLE #9:
Demand Evidence of Growth

Most of the leadership training programs I have examined evaluated their success in terms of how much information or how many experiences students had been offered.

A more appropriate approach is to value the process according to evidence suggesting that the emerging leaders "own" the information, concepts, relationships, and behaviors that the process was developed to provide. This is known in some circles as "competency-based training." This means that a person has only been trained if there are tangible indicators of enhanced leadership competencies in his or her performance as a leader.

"SYNERGIC" DEVELOPMENT

In developing the competencies of leaders, there are certain ingredients that, when combined, create discernible synergy. Truthfully, I have found very few ministries that have consciously and strategically incorporated all of these elements into a productive process. However, those ministries that have done so not only generate dozens and dozens of great leaders, but also wow pastors and other ministry analysts who examine the process that produced those leaders.

While there is no single program that will work for every ministry, the experience of these groundbreaking leadership incubators defines the most necessary and useful building blocks that can be designed into any ministry's developmental process.

Research on leadership development has underscored the importance of combining four particular facets of growth:

1. The *personal development* of the leader (addressing needs, interests, and self-esteem);

2. *a clear concept* of leadership itself;

3. actionable and reliable *feedback;* and

4. *skill building.*

Research suggests that until a potential leader has a personal break-through—that is, a sense of peace with self, and the ability to identify and work through personal barriers to leading effectively—all the training in the world will leave the emerging leader incomplete and frustrated. Bearing in mind the nine developmental principles just described, here are some of the elements that could be profitably included within the training procedures undertaken by any ministry.[2]

Self-Evaluation

Before individuals can hope to grow, they must have a realistic under-standing of who they are. This encompasses factors such as strengths, weak-nesses, style, fears, goals, gifts, talents, and role preferences.

Ministries often identify future leaders through one of two means. The most common is reliance upon the intuitive assumptions of existing leaders to discover potential leaders. The other approach is to allow individuals to position themselves as potential leaders.

There are some significant disadvantages to these methods. Having an inaccurate or incomplete understanding of others or of ourselves can lead us to make bad choices when choosing potential leaders. We may be fooled into believing someone is a candidate for leadership by their self-confidence, their ability to communicate effectively, or their economic success in the market-place. Sometimes we can even fool ourselves into thinking we're something that we're not—especially when it is something we would like to be, or to be seen as by other people.

To prevent this from happening, the most effective training programs utilize various tests and assessment tools. Some of the most useful of those tools include the following:

The Meyers-Briggs Type Indicator is a simple test that describes one's personality and interaction type. The test provides four classifications based upon how an individual relates to the world; the dominant mode of perceiving reality; the preference of structure and order or of flexibility and spontaneity; and whether the primary basis for decisions is logic- or values-based.

Because of the many studies conducted on the applicability of this test to organizational behavior, the MBTI is one of the more useful resources.

The Personal Profile System, commonly known as the DiSC test, provides an analysis of personal behavior and interaction patterns. Popular among ministries, this tool offers an assessment based upon perceptions of the behavior expected by others, instinctive responses to pressure, and self-perceptions.

The Wagner-Modified Houts Questionnaire is a means of estimating which of the twenty-seven spiritual gifts God may have given to an individual. Leadership is only one of these gifts. This test has helped thousands of people who want to be active in ministry focus their efforts more productively by clarifying their areas of giftedness and how to pursue appropriate service.

The Leadership Practices Inventory is a self-administered survey that uses a person's answers to thirty questions to identify how well an individual performs in each of five core leadership dimensions deemed by the LPIs creators to be the keys to effective leadership. Those five keys relate to being a change agent, inspiring a shared vision, empowering others, modeling, and encouraging.

The Ministry Leadership Profile provides an analysis of a person's calling, gifts, and competencies in relation to leadership. Using a 360-degree feedback system in which people who know the person being evaluated provide their input based upon their past experience with the person, the MLP is designed to determine the likelihood that a person is called to leadership, identify areas of strength and weakness in character, and suggest strengths and weaknesses in critical leadership skills. This series of tests is specifically related to leadership in Christian ministry.

The Role Preference Inventory is a self-evaluation that helps individuals choose their preferred leadership role within the aggregate ministry framework. Based on answers to ten simple questions, this test places people in one of three primary roles. There are those capable of being a "captain," described as people who accept responsibility, can handle intense pressure, and thrive on making the final decision. "Developers and managers" are identified as people who get involved in the decision making but need a superior to report to and gain guidance from. The remaining group is the "strong players," individuals who make significant contributions to the group's activities but do not want the responsibility and pressure embraced by the other two types.

No matter which tool (or tools) you use, it is invaluable to incorporate some type of objective, market-tested resource to provide a leader with objective context about his or her standing as a leader. Once insights have been gleaned regarding a person's capacity and potential, then targeted training can be designed and implemented.

Whether the tests and profiles utilized have been selected by the ministry or by the leader is irrelevant. The greatest value of these tools is that they provide unbiased, impersonal assessments of the current standing and future potential of an individual who believes he or she may be called to serve God through leadership.

Environmental Analysis

The success of all leaders depends upon their ability to read the cultural conditions around them. Environmental analysis is one of the core competencies of a great leader. Living in the Age of Information has facilitated capturing insights into the present nature and evolution of our culture. But the trick to effective leadership is going beyond the mere ownership of information to knowing what to make of it.

The most important question a leader must be able to answer regarding conditions and changes in the ministry environment is "So what?" Reading articles, newsletters, periodicals, and books related to cultural change, public opinion, national religious beliefs and practices, and ministry trends will keep a leader informed. Observing people and organizations in action will provide additional clues. Interacting with people on issues germane to the health and future of the Church will introduce further data for consideration. But the information must result in actionable ideas.

Toward that end, leaders must shift from focusing on "what" to "So what?" Developing a list of challenging questions that will guide the Church into a productive, transforming future will help. Some of those questions might be the following:

- How has decentralization within our culture affected my ministry?

- What types of programs and ministries can we effectively offer busy people?

- What are the most important needs that people are expecting churches to address?

- How can my ministry be restructured to respond in rapid and appropriate ways?

- What are the emerging needs in people's lives that we should anticipate, enabling us to provide solutions at the point of need?

- What are other ministries learning about change strategies that could help us conceptualize a more effective change process in our ministry?

- What types of demographic changes are occurring in our community that will reshape our ministry?

- How are the needs, expectations, and concerns of our key audience niches changing?

- If we had additional resources, what would be the most strategic application of those resources given our opportunities and vision?

These are just a few of the questions that ought to be common points of reflection and discussion among existing and emerging leaders within the Church. Constantly collecting information and analyzing it in terms of direct ministry implications is a necessary skill for all leaders.

Vision

While there are some leaders whose primary focus is the discernment and communication of vision, every true leader must have a deep understanding of the vision for his or her ministry. Without a clear vision in mind, there is no place to lead the people.

Every leader should develop the ability to do three things related to vision.

First, they must be able to discern God's vision for their ministry. This entails an extended time of self-discovery, intense interaction with God, assessing the ministry environment, and gaining counsel from trusted advisers.[3]

When God raises up leaders, He has a specific vision for the people those leaders have been called to mobilize. Knowing God's vision for the ministry is the starting point for effectively leading people forward.

Second, a leader must be able to articulate the vision in ways that inspire and direct people. This entails developing a vision statement, which is a brief, punchy declaration of the unique purpose for which God has allowed that specific ministry to exist. The leader must use all available opportunities to cast that vision to the people who will make it come to pass.[4]

Finally, leaders must incorporate the vision into every aspect of the ministry. Progress is evaluated according to the vision. People are hired based on the ministry needs dictated by the vision. Sermon topics are selected in keeping with the vision. Strategic plans are determined by the content of the vision. Relationships with other ministries are developed in light of the vision. Vision, in short, becomes the centerpiece of the ministry—and of the leader's life.

Operating as a visionary is not natural for some people. Those who operate intuitively sometimes feel that articulating a specific vision unnecessarily encumbers the ministry. To persuade such individuals of the value of this aspect of leadership, a development program may:

- *Build gradually.* Each leader might be encouraged to create a vision statement for his or her own life, for his or her family, for a ministry within his church. Other leaders would then critique the language and comprehensiveness of the statement. They would not challenge the core content of the vision, since that is between God and the leader.

- *Direct the focus outward.* Challenge the emerging leader to describe the ministry's vision to people who have no connection with the ministry, to see how clear and compelling it comes across to those on the outside.

- *Direct the focus inward.* Leaders might be encouraged to identify future opportunities available to the ministry in light of the vision.

- *Get feedback from others.* Speak to groups of people connected with the ministry about the vision, to gain feedback from them as to how inspiring the presentation of the vision was to them.

- *Consider the alternative.* Examine past failures or setbacks within the ministry in light of the vision. The purpose of this exercise would be to determine how strategies, plans, and activities that stray from the vision diminish our potential.

Leaders are the recipients, carriers, and protectors of the vision. Endeavors that improve their ability to live the vision can only enhance their leadership and the strength and influence of the ministries they lead.

Motivating People

Leaders cannot get any significant job accomplished without the efforts of other people. But everyone has his or her own agenda in life. Leaders are able to motivate people to reshape their agendas and actively participate in the furtherance of the ministry's efforts. A great leader does not manipulate people through personal charisma, entrancing speeches, or empty promises. Great leaders motivate people through the delivery of honest substance.

To get people to follow, a leader must attract and inspire people. To refine an emerging leader's ability to motivate people, assign him or her a specific task that will require that leader to attract a team of people and get those people to sign on for the duration of the task. During the process, the change partner should evaluate the emerging leader's efforts at attracting people, bonding with them, communicating effectively, assigning tasks appropriately, clarifying expectations, supporting people adequately, and rejoicing in successes achieved.

It will be tempting to intrude in the process as it unfolds, but the best change partners allow the emerging leader to learn from mistakes—that is, by making note of those things the emerging leader does that could be enhanced in future efforts. Only if the emerging leader is headed for crisis or disaster should the change partner intercede.

WHAT EFFECTIVE LEADERS DO TO MOTIVATE PEOPLE

- Captivate their hearts and minds by addressing things that matter to them.
- Earn their respect by demonstrating godly character.
- Win their trust by delivering on your promises.
- Clearly and convincingly communicate your purpose: to serve them.
- Facilitate their enduring focus on a compelling vision.
- Offer them a concise, significant, and challenging role in the fulfillment of the vision.
- Support them with resources, guidance, encouragement, and rewards.
- Describe your reasonable performance expectations of them.
- Lead by offering captivating ideas, persuasive words, and an inspiring example.
- Always place the needs of the people above the needs of the program.
- Provide generous praise; selflessly and genuinely deflect credit to the entire team.
- Celebrate each small win along the path to ultimate victory.

Motivation based upon stirring public speaking is generally less effective than motivation drawn from vision, character, modeling, and personal interaction. Preparing leaders to motivate by who they are rather than what they say is a significant step in the development process. People are more likely to follow a leader because they trust and respect that person than because of excitement generated by a new idea or project that has been proposed by the leader. Motivation based entirely on an emotional high is typically short-lived; motivation based on belief in the leader and the vision has staying power.

Individuals who fail to inspire participation must evaluate why their calls to action fell upon deaf ears.

- Did they recruit the wrong people?
- Did they use the wrong message?

- Did they present the opportunity in a way that was too dry, confusing or unattractive?

- Is there a perceived dissonance between what the leader says and does that might cause people not to trust or respect him or her?

- Was there an adequate base of resources and support to ensure success?

- Was the goal unrealistic?

- Was the connection between the task and the ministry's vision sufficiently visible?

A leader without followers is merely a solo performer. And a leader whose followers lend halfhearted support is destined for hardship, disappointment, and failure. If you plan to prepare a leader for success and enable him to maximize his or her potential, helping the leader develop effective motivational skills is a necessity.

Mobilizing People

The last thing any of us want to do is waste time. If we have bought into a vision for ministry and are motivated to get involved, we trust our leaders to coordinate matters to maximize our personal investment of time, energy, and expertise.

Mobilization requires the ability to assemble the right people to accomplish necessary tasks; to organize those people and coordinate their efforts; and to equip them to carry out their duties with excellence. Effective mobilization requires a certain amount of planning to determine how people, time, and resources will be used; how these goals will be communicated in a focused and timely manner; and how people will be trained to do their assigned jobs.

Change partners may have the opportunity to evaluate the emerging leader's readiness in all of these areas. Again, lecturing an emerging leader on mobilization practices, or allowing him or her to observe another leader mobilizing believers is one thing. Taking full responsibility for the act of mobilizing people is another.

After there has been sufficient discussion and consideration of mobilization techniques and challenges, providing the emerging leader with a "live" opportunity to mobilize the laity for ministry action is the best learning experience available. As always, it is best to start with a small assignment— that is, relatively few people engaged in a short-term project that will have limited consequences. Such endeavors provide low-risk opportunities to put theory into practice and to learn from mistakes while causing little damage. As the emerging leader masters a challenge, progressively larger and more significant challenges can be entrusted to his or her care.

Developing Strategy

Great leaders think and behave strategically. One of the most challenging elements in leadership development is to get an emerging leader to consistently think and act in strategic ways.

This facet of the development process may require a greater degree of intensive, front-end attention than any other element in the process. Case studies in which emerging leaders are given scenarios and asked to prescribe a strategic response, are critiqued by a mentor, and are further informed by the case outcome are very useful tools. Evaluating the strategic plans of various ministries may also provide some useful experience in thinking strategically. Eventually, creating a strategic plan or, less burdensome, working through a strategic response to certain eventualities facing the ministry will improve the individual's strategic mind.

In assessing the ability of the individual to anticipate and respond strategically, there are several keys to growth.

First, help emerging leaders identify their assumptions. We all possess assumptions that form the foundation of our initial perceptions and responses. Some of these assumptions are valid and helpful, but many are erroneous and harmful. Identifying those assumptions and then discerning which are valid greatly improves the prospects of decision makers arriving at appropriate conclusions.

Next, examine how thoroughly and intelligently the individual has assessed his or her ministry environment. Decisions are made within a framework of understanding; good decisions cannot be made unless the individual has accumulated, dissected, and wisely interpreted strategic information.

Piecing together relevant bits of data is difficult; there is always more information available than is useful, and there are often valuable bits of insight that seem unattainable. Strategic thinkers use the available information, plus their intuition, to develop a comprehensive understanding of the situations at hand and how to influence people and circumstances to move toward the vision. Honing these analytical skills will prove to be invaluable.

Third, some energy might be profitably devoted to understanding past efforts and outcomes. A great strategist has no interest in reinventing history, or in repeating others' mistakes. While conditions have undoubtedly changed, discovering principles, obstacles, and alternatives from historical precedent can be of great help.

Before a strategic leader can move forward, two more considerations must be addressed. One is identifying the base of resources that can be called upon for the benefit of the Church. The other is to conceptualize and reflect upon all of the possible responses to the situation at hand. Acting strategically then becomes an easier challenge. Having identified the plausible alternatives and estimated their likely outcomes, the best decisions can be made for the good of the entire ministry.

In developing strategic thinking capabilities, use as many practical experiences as possible. Examine how corporations are handling threats and opportunities in the marketplace, and attempt to determine what strategic thinking led to their choices—and based on real-world outcomes, how aptly they behaved. Work in concert with church leaders to imagine the scenarios that could transpire, arriving at actionable conclusions, then following the outcome of those conclusions and doing a postmortem on the experience.

Team Building

Great leaders are team players. Their success depends entirely upon their ability to attract, equip, guide, and retain talented and gifted people to achieve outcomes that bless other people. Even though one of the cornerstones of ministry is to establish community, and despite the fact that most people recognize the importance of cooperative efforts, creating a healthy and effective team is one of the most difficult and taxing challenges faced by a leader.

Team building is a multifaceted art. Initially it requires an understanding of the different roles that must be filled by team members. The leader must then assess the talents and gifts of the people whom he or she has attracted, conceptualizing an appropriate role for each person. The leader must simultaneously develop a web of meaningful relationships among the role players built upon trust and interdependence. This intimates that the leader must keep his or her people sensitized to relationships, not just tasks.

The leader is also responsible for preparing each team member for success and must deftly weave together the various talents and skills of the players to move the team toward achieving its goals. This entails conversations and interactions designed to challenge team members to operate at a higher level of performance.

Encouraging communication is another major function of a team builder, since the lack of significant communication often leads to misunderstandings and conflicts that can destroy effective ministry and personal growth. In the end, the team is strengthened not only by its successes but also by the natural but intentional celebration of those wins. The team builder thus serves as the chief cheerleader for the group.

If your ministry has the ability to create safe team-building exercises—strategic games played among emerging leaders (such as mock presentations, paint wars, rock climbing, low-competition sports events, political strategy exercises)—then emerging leaders can experience the ups and downs of the process before their efforts matter. Even simple role-playing games can provide opportunities to try out different strategies.

Many ministries develop people's team-building abilities by having them lead loosely knit issue-oriented groups of people—committees, commissions, study groups, change coalitions—toward becoming productive contributors rather than destructive snipers. Having a senior leader frequently checking in with the team builder is an important safeguard that enables the emerging leader to stay focused on the big picture and not get swallowed up by the myopia of the typical group.

One of the toughest tasks to teach a team builder is when and how to give a healthy team its freedom. Once a team finds its identity, personality, and rhythm, it is ready for greater independence. If the team builders are doing their jobs, new leaders will be ready to replace them. This will enable the first team builder to use his or her talents in other needed situations. The ministry's senior leaders and change partners can be instrumental in guiding this aspect of the developmental process.

Reinforcement

You've heard the axioms.

- *"People live up to your expectations."*
- *"You get what you reward."*
- *"If you don't enforce it, you out force it."*
- *"An ounce of encouragement compensates for a pound of frustration."*
- *"If it's worth doing right, it's worth celebrating when it's done right."*

Triteness notwithstanding, these expressions are useful reminders that an effective leader is more than a courageous, wise, forward-thinking motivator. Leaders must also be cheerleaders.

As emotional beings, we respond to reinforcement. The leader must underscore those ideas and behaviors that benefit the aggregate ministry or God's kingdom. The leader is in a better position than anyone to perceive the things that are worthy of recognition. And the leader is also best suited, by virtue of his or her standing in the hierarchy, to provide meaningful feedback.

Putting It All Together

Make no mistake about it: Developing the entire leadership package in an individual is a difficult, draining, long-term challenge. One reason why many ministries have fared so poorly in developing leaders is that they have not sustained a total commitment to the process. If you are serious about seeing leaders raised up in your ministry vineyard, you must make the commitment.

Although an emerging leader must provide the driving force behind his or her own developmental program, it is the responsibility of senior leaders in the emerging leader's church to ensure that a reasonable and comprehensive approach is undertaken. While there is no "perfect" program, and none that will meet everyone's needs, let me describe the approach that has been most effective for some of the leading ministries.

The process starts with tests geared to determining the nature and needs of the prospective leader. The results of such assessments provide direction for the next phase: a customized training process. The design will determine the sequence of activities, the appropriate players in the process, and the logical emphases given the individual to be trained.

The training itself should incorporate four distinct strategies: classroom experience; interactive group experiences; intensive one-to-one mentoring or coaching by a senior leader; and on-the-job training. The classroom time should involve lectures, discussions, videos, or computer-driven instruction and case studies. The group interaction is maximized by a combination of role-playing and outdoor team-building adventures.

This overview assumes that a ministry will be simultaneously developing the leadership character and competencies of several individuals. That is desirable not only because it guarantees a larger number of incoming leaders to guide the ministry, but also because it allows the ministry to exploit economies of scale and to avail trainees of valuable group experiences.

THE PASTOR AS TRAINER

Here's a final word on the training process. Many people assume that, within a church context, the lead trainer should be the senior pastor. Given our previous discussion about the nature and skills of today's senior pastors, this assumption is obviously counterproductive.

Senior pastors who are truly leaders will enjoy nurturing additional leaders for ministry. However, senior pastors who are teachers by gifting will enjoy talking about leadership, but their limited credibility and lack of true insight on the topic will not produce the most effective leaders, since the developmental process is more about observation and experience than it is about lectures and theory.

Pastors whose primary gift is administration will help emerging leaders understand some of the organizational facets of leading but will leave trainees malnourished in the visionary and strategic ends of the job.

Through their words and deeds, pastors who major on shepherding will communicate the importance of caring for people, but they will fail in preparing leaders who can fulfill the more intellectual ends of the job.

If the church has a senior pastor who is not a gifted leader, he or she may add value to the developmental process by applying their talent in the circumspect areas they master. However, they would benefit the church and the trainees by assigning leadership of the development process to a more leadership-sensitive individual.

Our primary goal must be to enable the Church to maximize life transformation. This requires that we provide ministries with an ample supply of called, gifted, and competent leaders. Combating the powers of darkness in this world requires the intelligent preparation and deployment of the literally millions of individuals whom God has ordained to be Christian leaders. Keeping the Church strong by fortifying the ranks of its leaders will continue to be an ongoing need in the community of faith.

And yet, quantity is not enough. We must commit ourselves to the process of leadership development so that we empower leaders to succeed. It's one thing to give leaders an opportunity; it's another thing altogether to set them up for success. As we equip leaders to lead people to victory, encouraging believers everywhere to fully utilize their God-given gifts, we may yet experience God's merciful hand of healing and restoration as He ushers in the second coming of the Church.

THIRTEEN

REENGINEERING THE LOCAL CHURCH

THERE IS AN OLD SAYING that the things that got you to where you are today are not the things that will get you to where you need to be tomorrow. That adage represents wise and timely counsel to the Church. In this era of rapid and profound change, we know that the shape of the Church must change significantly if it is to remain both alive and influential. The likely structural changes that will redefine the Church must be taken seriously. We must be prepared to reengineer the contours of ministry without compromising its content.

If we wish to maximize our influence by restructuring the Church for optimum effectiveness, we need to consider the following perspectives as guiding concepts.

First, we must have a clear goal in mind as we set out to develop the new Church. Our ultimate goal is to empower people to become transformed followers of Jesus Christ. This means that we must provide processes, resources, and relationships that facilitate the communication, acceptance, and pursuit of moral and spiritual truth, growth in godly character, significant participation in a community of faith, and a deepening and passionate relationship with God.

Our primary source of guidance must be the Bible. But a careful reading of the Bible provides us with plentiful direction related to theology and character development, yet almost no restrictions on structures and methods. I always thought it significant that Jesus never directly addressed the necessary contours of Church structure. His unwavering attention was devoted to beliefs, values, relationships, and behavior—not organizational development.

This suggests that, while the ends do not always justify the means, we have more leeway than many believers have assumed.

And yet, our freedom to innovate is not absolute. We must always assess the suitability and value of our innovations in light of our ultimate purpose. Whether we eliminate an existing process or create a new approach, we must determine if that action is geared to building God's kingdom, or if it is primarily designed to further our own ends. If our effort results in positive forward movement for God's ends, and can be accomplished without compromising His values, principles, and standards, then it is permissible. Anything short of that is indefensible.

Innovation alone is inadequate. We are also responsible for operating strategically, responding appropriately within our cultural context. For instance, we must acknowledge that niche marketing, rather than mass marketing, is the future. There will always be exceptions to every rule, and full-service mega-churches represent a high-profile exception to the niche principle. However, megachurches are not the wave of the future, although they will be integral in developing the future Church.

If we are to maintain momentum and influence, we must build on existing islands of strength. Congregations are currently our best organizational resource. As we develop the Church of the future, our best strategy will be to grow the new formations from the resources and assistance provided by these present hubs of strength.

Ultimately, the moral and spiritual revolution that will produce the new Church will emerge from among the laity. The impetus to change and the creative focus and force reside among the frustrated masses, not among the distracted professionals. Marrying the resources of both the laity and the clergy could introduce an exciting era of Christian renewal. But the catalyst for this new reformation will be the people, not the professionals.

Other changes must occur as well. While it is true that certain things cannot and must not change—for example, the Bible has been and always will be the standard for the Church—there are some significant transitions that will have to take place in the emerging Church:

Change factor:	Changing from:	Changing to:
Authority	centralized	decentralized
Leadership	pastor-driven	lay-driven
Power distribution	vertical	horizontal
Reaction to change	resistance	acceptance
Identity	tradition and order	mission and vision
Scope of ministry	all-purpose	specialized
Practices	tradition bound	relevance bound
People's role	observation and support	participation and innovation
Principal product	knowledge	transformation
Success factors	size, efficiency, image	accessibility, impact, integrity
Primary challenges	momentum, relationships, leadership, complacency	heresy, relationships, unity, leadership, balance
Effect of technology	attention-grabbing	growth facilitating
Means to growth	more, better-run programs	more relationships and experiences
Growth prospects	limited	unlimited

As we introduce new approaches to ministry, many of the fundamental elements of the Church will undoubtedly be redefined. As this chart suggests, the net effect of the changes will be to make the Church more responsive and proactive, without jeopardizing the core values and truths upon which the Church is based. Structures, formats, styles, and relationships can be adapted to fit the Church's goals and standards, regardless of past prohibitions and the existing expectations held by many people.

Naturally, the various changes that take place will have a variety of effects. Every change introduces an element of danger to those affected by the change. We can be reasonably certain, though, that many of the changes that will be introduced into the emerging Church will produce greater ministry capacity than exists at present. For instance, some of the new forms of the Church, such as the cyberchurch, will allow us to penetrate entire segments of the population that are currently inaccessible to us.

Some changes promoted by the emerging Church will produce a different ministry environment, without necessarily improving it. Changing the times of public ministry events from Sunday morning to a variety of times throughout the week is one such change: Altering the ministry schedule does not necessarily upgrade the quality, the value, or the reach of ministry.

In other instances we may simply be trading one set of problems for another. One example may be the increasing influence of technology on our ministry experience. You can perhaps imagine some of the positive impacts (efficient delivery of information, more memorable communications, tacit message of relevance, broader distribution of the message, greater convenience). But you can probably imagine some drawbacks, too (increased ministry costs, ministry depersonalization, greater lead time required to prepare, loss of information control).

The changes produced by the emerging Church will also raise the potential for undesirable ministry consequences. The potential for heresy is heightened, for instance, when the decentralization of teaching occurs. Unless safeguards and accountability systems can be instituted, the shift from what exists to what will be the norm could create even worse headaches in such dimensions of ministry. That is why strategic action based on critical analysis, prayer, and problem anticipation is so crucial to the future of American Christianity.

These shifts should also cause us to question some of our current practices. For example, I have suggested that congregational bodies in the future will be decentralized and increasingly focused, rather than centralized and multidimensional. That must lead us to reevaluate the advisability of spending the billions of dollars presently being raised for the construction of new buildings, parking lots, and other institutional monuments.

Although the development of classrooms, multipurpose facilities, and other bricks-and-mortar products is not inherently indefensible, when we can easily foresee the potential of an era in which "big is bad," good stewardship calls us to carefully examine the long-term wisdom of a significant capital campaign. At the very least, we must reconceptualize how Christians will use space in the decades ahead if the Church has become decentralized and niche-oriented.

FOUR IMPORTANT TRANSITIONS CHURCHES MUST MAKE

Let me outline four specific ways in which a typical congregation might transition "into an effective twenty-first-century ministry."

1. Birthing Centers for New Churches

Church planting is a popular ministry activity. But almost all of the churches that are being initiated are following the congregational model. These are clearly churches being planted not for future growth, but for present-day maintenance. A congregation that wants to invest in the future of God's kingdom would allocate its church planting resources to the initiation of new-style churches.

Cyberchurch planting. One example of appropriate church birthing would be to create a virtual church on the Internet. I am not referring to the Web sites that several thousand churches now have in place. The vast majority of these sites are nothing more than on-line advertisements for the physical church, along with a tour of the church archives. The nonrelational nature of such sites does nothing to inspire an individual to get connected to God and His people.

Instead of locking people in the on-line church archives and expecting them to read sermon texts, theological arguments, and other scholarly documents, the existing church could turn its computer-savvy people loose on developing a site that would stimulate and excite them if they were searching for spiritual meaning and connections. Sites could include:

• Relational options—chat rooms and bulletin boards;

- spiritual experiences—live worship music, downloaded audio clips of worship music, video clips of valuable teaching, or visuals of spiritually significant places;
- points of access for spiritual events as well as other useful sites and resources.

Why would we want to do this? Based on our research, I have projected that by the year 2010, 10 to 20 percent of Americans will derive all their spiritual input (and output) through the Internet. Just a decade from now, as many as fifty million people will choose to grow spiritually without ever stepping onto a church campus again. Staying ahead of this trend presents almost limitless ministry opportunities and enables us to reach people that might otherwise never hear the transforming message of the gospel.

House church planting. The house church has emerged as yet another model vying for people's participation. The house church appeals to Americans because it fits our culture: It is decentralized, has a horizontal structure, exerts low control and authority over its participants, and operates without historical traditions. House churches offer convenience in scheduling and location, are highly relational, and do not waste money on buildings and overhead. They represent the ultimate in flexibility.

Accompanying these valued characteristics, though, are some frightening compensating realities that the Church must find a way to address if this innovative model is going to succeed. For instance, unless we train biblically literate, skilled teachers, what will prevent heresy from spreading like wildfire among these small bodies of religious explorers? Without a group of leaders trained in motivation, facilitation, vision casting, resource development, and conflict resolution, what will be the average tenure of a house church participant? Apart from a grassroots uprising, how will Christian community be developed? Lacking individuals skilled in worship facilitation, how often will most people worship a God whom they barely know about and rarely experience?

As a sponsor for a house church, the congregational church could be an invaluable support source for this independent offshoot. Examples of parent church "blessings" could include:

- providing access to congregational resources;

- developing procedures to maintain accountability;

- overseeing the efficient dispensing of funds raised for the house church; and

- connecting the group with other house churches in the area (if desired).

The house church would maintain complete autonomy in terms of its leadership, decision-making, and ministry activities. The congregational church would simply represent a base of security and a spiritual touchstone that would remain available should the house church have a related need. Undoubtedly, some house churches would appreciate being blessed or "sanctioned" by a "mother" church.

Other alternatives. There will be a variety of other new forms of ministry that represent emerging trends in the future of the Church and could very well replace the ill-fated congregational model. Examples of these include *independent, community-wide celebration events.* Fed up with the programming, the politics, the mentality, and the lifelessness of congregational churches, individuals or small groups of Christians hungry to experience God's presence will independently create and sponsor worship events open to the public. Offered on an irregular basis, these events will feature the best speakers, musicians, and other creative talent that money can buy because the underlying purpose is to have a memorable experience with God, not to build an institution.

Another emerging model will be *dialogical forums,* an extension of the Christian coffeehouses that dot the landscape and attract twenty-somethings these days. These forums will be akin to the apostle Paul's public square debates, but the atmosphere will be more congenial, less confrontational, and more dispassionately interactive. People will come together for a time of discussion regarding religious-oriented matters, listening to anyone who wishes to offer their views, maybe even occasionally inserting their own perspectives.

Expect to see *compassion clusters* arise. These will be small groups of people who share a common desire to reach out and help others, as their form of in-reach and outreach. They will represent a bridge between secular, non-profit organizations that perform charitable deeds and Christian parachurch ministries, which are organized to provide funds, policies, benefits, and other parameters for those aligned with the ministry. The distinctive of compassion clusters is that the times when those groups get together to minister to people in need will represent the aggregate church experience.

It's too early to say much about other forms that are already showing up on our radar: *marketplace meetings, uni-focus ministry groups,* and *interfaith events.* You can count on a myriad of new models taking shape over the next few years.

2. Training Centers

As noted throughout this book, one of the benefits of the congregational church is its potential for identifying and training leaders and teachers. The emerging decentralized Church will have a voracious need for Christians with these gifts.

By repositioning the congregational church to be "boot camps" for these gifted people, the congregational entity would be assured of a lasting role by virtue of its emphasis on the importance of Bible knowledge and spiritual direction. Seminaries could have embraced this role, but have generally chosen to remain professional certification agencies. Thus, teaching churches could fill the gap in teacher training and the absence of leadership development could be addressed by training churches. Naturally, the individuals whose skills and gifts have been honed by the congregational church would then have numerous options as to how to best serve God—and one of those options would be to utilize their abilities within the congregational body.

3. Service Centers

One of the marks of the true Church is its involvement in the lives of needy people. A decentralized group, such as those who attend house churches or cyberchurches, may have difficulty figuring out how to devote time, expertise, and resources to compassionate ministry. Thus, another significant role for the congregational church is to act as a clearinghouse for service opportunities.

The congregational body might coordinate the active ministry efforts of people from a broad base within the community, using its Web site (as well as other, more standard communications methods) to promote upcoming chances for involvement in ministry. Various lay ministries such as soup kitchens, home building, health clinics, clothing drives, Big Brother/Big Sister projects, short-term missions trips, and the like could be instigated by the congregation but intentionally opened up to a broader community of Christians.

4. Partnerships

Yet another strategy for congregational churches to pursue is to enter into strategic partnerships or alliances with other ministries—including parachurch ministries.

For many years there has been an uneasy existence between the local church and parachurch organizations. Local churches have been wary of parachurch groups taking the time, money, energy, and attention of church members. Parachurch agencies have sometimes shown little respect for the ministry efforts of churches, especially when those efforts were in the building stage.

But the average Christian doesn't care about which organization gets credit, or institutional loyalty. People have very limited resources and are focused on the bottom line rather than on peripheral matters. It is time to eliminate territorial battles between churches and parachurch groups and to focus on kingdom outcomes. In the coming years congregational churches may find that they can achieve their vision more effectively by pruning their own roster of programs, downsizing staff, and working in tandem with parachurch ministries that specialize in specific ministry endeavors.

There are many advantages to this process, among them the reduction of congregational overhead and liabilities, the expansion of the community of saints beyond the walls of the congregation, and the decentralization of the congregational entity (without jeopardizing the focus).

All of these benefits sound theoretically wonderful and spiritually commendable. However, the real test of a congregation committed to the evolution of the Church may be its involvement in promoting alternative forms of ministry. When there is evidence of existing, traditional churches helping people to get connected to alternative church formats, instead of making their total commitment of time, talent, and treasure to the congregational body, then we can be confident that the Church is moving toward health.

THINK OF WHAT IT MEANS

As these changes become more commonplace and the emerging Church picks up steam, many major transitions will be triggered, both organizationally and personally. Don't set yourself up for culture shock! Let's identify some of the inevitable outcomes now, so that you can ponder and be prepared for those outcomes.

Traditional ministry organizations and roles will be redefined. Denominational headquarters will be repositioned as resource centers, and denominations themselves will hold a much less significant place on the religious map. There will be fewer full-time, career ministry professionals, since ministry responsibility will be increasingly accepted and executed by lay believers.

Representatives of the new Church and parachurch agencies will have to assume a higher public profile as more and more existing congregational churches are closed down and the remaining congregations have a diminished capacity for handling the life crises of people unconnected to the Church.

Admissions to Bible colleges and Christian colleges will rise steadily as individuals associated with Christianity recognize that these schools provide much of the theological education and lifestyle shaping that the congregational church did not provide.

The role of the family will be greatly elevated in the faith dimension. As individuals begin to cultivate a greater sense of responsibility for their own spiritual development, this will affect family life as well. As parents' minds and hearts are influenced by God's principles, their behavior will be affected, which in turn will influence the thinking and actions of their children.

At least initially, we can expect to see a decline in ministry performance as competition explodes for people's involvement. After a period of filtering, the reliable ministries will emerge, and quality in ministry performance will rise.

People's true spiritual nature will emerge. Many people, stripped of the spiritual "safety net" that many congregational churches provided, will decide to get serious about their faith and become personally active. Others will see the reduced omnipresence of churches as an invitation to relax their spiritual quest and underlying sense of guilt, settling into a state of spiritual lethargy. Still others, burned by their early-life church experiences or disappointed by their adult fling with churches, will seek the divine through other means.

Midsize churches will struggle more than larger and smaller churches. The typical midsize church will have difficulty maintaining its equilibrium, being neither highly relational in nature nor having a sufficient quality and breadth of niche ministries.

IMPORTANT CONSIDERATIONS FOR
EFFECTIVE CROSS-GENERATIONAL MINISTRY

In addition to developing entirely new models of the church, recent and forthcoming cultural changes demand that we reassess some of the methods we utilize within the new ministry structures. For instance, the ways in which we communicate with people must be scrutinized for effectiveness. This will be especially crucial as Baby Busters and Mosaics become more prolific and emerge as target populations for the Church.

Young adults increasingly have a tendency to integrate disparate information into new perspectives on reality. Educational psychologists tell us that today's young people are "mosaic thinkers," able to put information together in new patterns, often arriving at unusual, novel, or surprising conclusions. This is in contrast to Boomers, Builders, and Seniors who are "linear thinkers," assembling facts in a predictable path and generally arriving at predictable conclusions.

Their heavy diet of mass media, combined with the uncritical embrace of computer technologies and the national shift in morals and values, has resulted in an entirely new filter through which Americans receive and interpret information. Whether we applaud or oppose that filter is not the issue at hand: The mere emergence of the new filter mandates a new style of sermon or lesson development and delivery.

In fact, we have discovered that the younger the adult, the less interested he or she is in a smooth presentation. Excellence and professionalism are "performance strategies" that appeal to the late Builders and early Boomers. Among the Busters, however, the keys are relevance, genuineness, and authenticity. They are more interested in experiencing a sincere and honest presentation that raises meaningful questions than a polished, well-rehearsed speech that provides all the answers. Presenters who address the audience without constant reference to notes, and those who do not "hide" behind a pulpit, also seem to generate a more positive response from their listeners.

The younger churchgoers also look for different substance in Bible-related lessons. For instance, we have learned that younger adults resonate with "visionary preaching": that is, sermons that are not narrowly focused on the here and now, but that empower the listener to envision a better future, which they may play a role in creating and enjoying. The communications strategy that has most effectively overcome their aversion to moral absolutes has been the intelligent use of stories as the means of conveying truth. Stories, to the postmodernist, relativistic mind, are undeniable: Experience is permitted where theology or philosophy is rejected.

Increasingly we find that young people view sermons as lectures, or class presentations, and are one-sided communiqués that are ineffective. Churches that have experimented with interactive learning times, dialogical sermons, and other forms of Socratic communication are hitting a resonant chord among younger adults. To the Buster mind, participation in the process of learning and arriving at truths or principles is even more crucial than the truths or principles themselves. Naturally, this both threatens and baffles the typical older adult or those who are less open-minded.

More and more spiritual seekers, both committed Christians and new sojourners, are searching for preachers who come from the Bill Clinton school of preaching: empathetic public speaking ("I feel your pain"). Naturally, if this does not simultaneously evince a sense of vulnerability and compassion along with street-grown wisdom, people reject the presentation as an act, a piece of staged religiosity and manipulation. However, those who communicate with true sensitivity and depth serve as magnets to a pair of generations (Boomers and Busters) that are admittedly emotionally damaged and relationally starved.

Using excessive quotes, historical references, or literary references in sermons turns off young listeners. The use of quotes from esteemed individuals serves little purpose: The credibility lent by the quoted figure is not likely to be appreciated or accepted by the younger audience.

Remember, too, that scriptural references may not have the intended impact upon young listeners. Relatively few of the Busters and late Boomers know the names of the books of the Bible or even the most basic or popular scriptural passages. While the Word of God instructs, pierces, and empowers us, if carelessly used in teaching a biblically illiterate audience it may also unnecessarily discourage or repulse the listener—not because of the content of the Word, but because of how such references were used in the communication.

Finally, consider another factor that could impair your ability to influence young adults through preaching. When a young adult attends a church these days, it is not likely that he or she will return the following week. What does this do for the teacher or preacher who likes to use topical series that build upon one another? Consistency in attendance is a cultural artifact in America.

As you mull over these perspectives and related findings, keep this in mind: I am not asking you to like this reality, or to embrace it with open arms. I'm simply saying that for the sake of the Church, and for your own impact in ministry, we must deal with this reality intelligently, strategically, and intentionally. It is not an illusion, and it will not go away if we ignore it.

At first, all of these changes will strike us all hard. We have had a predictable, comfortable, secure ministry environment for so long that any changes will at first seem radical, sometimes even threatening. But as time progresses, we will recognize just how incredibly healthy many of the transitions have been for the Christian body at large and for us individually.

Whether you choose to remain involved in the congregational mold or to venture into the spiritual unknown, to experience the competing dynamics of independence and responsibility, move ahead boldly. God's perspective is that the structures and routines you engage with matter much less than the character and commitments that define you.

Can you find a spiritual environment that will consistently challenge you, encourage you, and facilitate your development in Christ? What commitments and attitudes will you have in relation to the emerging Church? Your choices in this arena matter, but only because they influence your relationship with God. Are you prepared for the coming era of transformation?

[FOURTEEN]
THE SPECIAL ROLE OF THE FAMILY

ABRAHAM LINCOLN ONCE PROCLAIMED, "The strength of a nation lies in the homes of its people." In that sense, things have not changed in the hundred-plus years since Lincoln made that observation. As we plunge into the twenty-first century, perhaps the most important resource we have is our families.

The second coming of the Church is all about renewing our ideas, our commitments, and our practices related to serving God and His creation. Unless we can

- Generate a nation full of believers who possess a healthy and comprehensive *biblical worldview,*

- prepare and release *true leaders* to direct our path, and

- facilitate the development *of new and vibrant ministry models* for the delivery of the Gospel message,

. . . the Church has little immediate future in America.

These three keys to converting the American church from a well-intentioned but powerless institution into the major agency of positive life transformation hinges on the performance of the family.

Many have written off the family as an anachronism. While it is true that our concept of "family" has been dramatically reshaped in the past three decades, the family remains the fundamental building block of our society. You and I are the products of our families; the media, the schools, the government, the marketplace, and even our friends can only influence us as much as our families allow us to be shaped by those entities. For better or worse, the family remains the cornerstone of human development.

If the Church is to have a future in America, and if that future at all resembles the kind of design I have outlined in the preceding pages, then the family will be at the center of the transitions that will create that future. This demands that we take the role of the family very seriously. The family is more than just an economic unit or a protective body; it is our primary educator. Through our families we learn about the important things: values, beliefs, acceptable behavior standards, self-esteem, and healthy relationships.

For the sake of the future Church, we must ensure that spiritual development remains one of the key elements that our families integrate into the mix of activities and goals to which they are committed. However, we must go far beyond where our families are today in their spiritual commitment. As we experience the decentralization of the Church in its traditional form, the family will necessarily have to absorb much of the spiritual responsibility that has usually been handled by congregations. Abdicating that responsibility to congregations and other external ministry entities was never a good idea in the first place; they have always been meant to supplement, not replace, the spiritual input and direction that God intended the family unit to provide within itself. But as we enter the new world of the Church, the role of the family will be even more significant.

CULTIVATING INTENTIONAL FAMILY SPIRITUALITY

In many ways, the family will be the heart of the new Church. Today the typical family picks up the spiritual pieces after family members have had their exposure to a church, a parachurch ministry, TV, school, and various marketplace experiences.

Each of those adventures leaves a mark on us, and it is expected that someone—perhaps a parent or other family member—will come along to tie those experiences and perspectives together. And that is exactly why families have little or no spiritual depth and coherence: We leave the brunt of the task of spiritual nurturing to external parties who have no personal knowledge of our background and needs, no plan, no strategy, and no back-end follow-up.

The only way in which the Church will thrive in the future is if families lead the process of directing and furthering their own spiritual growth. Changes within our culture have caused us to depend less and less upon churches to imprint our minds and hearts with God's truths and principles. For that reason we must commit to developing and implementing a spiritual development process and lifestyle.

Let me again emphasize this notion: *The future of the Church in America depends largely upon the spiritual commitment of families.* As intelligent and responsible adults, we must accept the privilege and obligation we have to lead our own households into God's presence, and then into the world armed with the mind of Christ.

The Grand Perspective

Each of us must come to see our family as the core spiritual unit. Just as religious education, worship, relationships, evangelism, stewardship, and service are key dimensions of church life, so they are crucial to the development of family life.

Parents in particular must understand the central role Christ has called the family unit to play in the aggregate framework of the true Church. Whether you attend a congregational church, or a house church, or are involved in other spiritual endeavors and relationships, the family is designed to be the foundational church unit. You may choose to incorporate your family into a larger church group, but your family is a church unto itself. Such a viewpoint demands that we reconsider the roles each of us plays within the family.[1]

Spiritual Headship

Most fathers think of themselves as economic providers for their wives and children, and perhaps as physical protectors. Most men have devoted surprisingly little time thinking about, and virtually no energy in planning for, what it means to be a father. Only a relative handful of fathers consciously and actively embrace the role of the spiritual head of the household.

This abdication of responsibility has serious consequences, for this role of spiritual headship is precisely the position the Bible calls every father to master. By being deeply committed to following Christ, men are called to lead their families into an equally deep and growing relationship with Christ.

While mothers tend to be more spiritually inclined than their husbands, only a minority of mothers place the spiritual nurturing of their families at the head of their list of important responsibilities. Given the cultural realities of America today, the mother shares a major role in the spiritual development of the children and in encouraging the spiritual advancement of her husband.

Together, husbands and wives must serve as the spiritual mentors of their children. For too long we have sloughed off the responsibilities of spiritually nurturing our children to anyone or any group that would take on that duty: Sunday schools, vacation Bible schools, midweek youth programs like Awana, Pioneer clubs, Young Life or Youth for Christ, or even media-driven influences such as Christian television or Christian videos. We have relied almost exclusively upon the efforts of others to train our children to be lovers of God.

At the same time, these organizations were never intended to provide the primary spiritual influence and education of our children. By abandoning their responsibility to guide their children in spiritual matters, parents across the nation have seriously stunted their children's spiritual growth.

With the decentralization of the Church in the coming millennium, it will be even more crucial that parents take back the spiritual leadership for their family. As parents we must reprioritize our lives, altering our perspectives and our schedules to reflect the primacy of family. We must, in fact, become spiritual leaders. That means adopting the character qualities and technical competencies of a true leader in order to mobilize, motivate, resource, and direct our families toward a common vision of knowing, loving, and serving God with all of our heart, mind, soul, and strength.

We must evaluate our efforts as spiritual leaders not in terms of whether or not we made it to a church service last Sunday, but in terms of how closely the quality of our lives conforms to the principles the Bible has exhorted us to achieve. We cannot rely upon the assistance of churches, parachurch ministries, the media, or Christian schools to do our work for us; we are the primary leaders, and they must build on the spiritual foundation we have provided for them.[2]

WHAT DOES SPIRITUAL FAMILY LEADERSHIP ENTAIL?

Our primary goal is to facilitate the development of a Christian community in America that possesses an influential, biblical worldview. In order to do this, we must cultivate the gifts of our members and practice Christian ministry in a way that is culturally and personally relevant and transforming.

How can families be involved? Here are a few ideas to stimulate your thinking.

Impart Christian Values

If we are responsible for developing the character of our children so that they mature into godly people, we must start young, taking every opportunity available to shape their minds and hearts. The best way to do this is through the deliberate, systematic teaching of Christian values.[3]

This is not the job of the Sunday school teacher; the teacher's task is to reinforce what we should have already communicated at home. Instilling appropriate values in our children is one of the best investments we can possibly make since those values influence the ways in which we see and respond to the world.

Perhaps the most powerful teaching "tool" at our disposal is our own example. Our family members learn best by observing what we do. This is one of the reasons why it is so critical that we embrace a biblical worldview; as our minds and hearts are influenced by God's principles, our behavior will be affected. That behavior then influences the thinking and actions of those who watch what we do.

We can also convey values through a direct course of education. Working with our family we may engage in activities that we have intentionally selected as a means to teach appropriate values (for example, abandoning the TV set for a few hours to work together at a soup kitchen, or taking time for family devotions). We may jointly analyze value-laden experiences, such as talking about the assumptions and values built into a movie or TV show, or reflecting on how someone has treated us and how we may properly respond.

Studying the Bible together, and purposefully searching for values and value-related lessons, is one of the elementary activities that facilitate our understanding of the values God expects us to embrace and demonstrate.

Teach the Bible

There is no substitute for a comprehensive knowledge of God's Word. Unless a family concentrates on growing in the knowledge of the Bible, their spiritual progress will be greatly impeded. Having regularly scheduled times when the family gets together to consider the lessons in specific passages is important. Memorizing verses together can be a fun and educational family adventure. Connecting the lessons into a worldview, by relating the lessons into a framework for perceiving the world and responding to daily challenges and opportunities, is a primary function of the family.

Develop Strong Relationships

Most Americans are confused about relationships. Many people, including professing Christians, have short-circuited the natural progression of emotional intimacy with their partners by engaging prematurely in sexual activity. Even within our families, we lack many basic communication skills: how to communicate effectively, how to resolve conflicts, and how to nurture and affirm others without being condescending or simplistic.

A major reason for our struggle in developing meaningful friendships is that we never had much coaching in this process ourselves, and we therefore do not know how to pass on useful information in this regard to our family members.

One of the most significant steps we can take toward achieving a healthy view of families is to invest large quantities of time in our family ties. The myth of quality time is just that—a myth. We cannot build deep, trusting, nurturing, lasting relationships, even with our own kin, unless we devote ample time to getting to know each other, to having shared experiences, and to consistently and lovingly nurturing each other. Again, we learn through experience and observation; what we model for our families is what they will take into the world as their own model for application.

Promote Christian Behavior

Biblical values and appropriate relationships will help us establish a lifestyle that honors God. However, parents must often take a proactive role in ensuring that children are behaving in ways that are consistent with scriptural principles.

The discussion of behaving Christianly, though, transcends merely reacting in the "right way" in a given situation. Beyond that it is imperative to model the significance of service—sacrificing some of our "free time" and disposable resources for the good of those who need our support. In our culture, we place a high value on service—being served, that is. Serving is viewed as the task of those who are inferior or subordinate. Given the biblical value that the greatest among us is he who views himself as the least among us, modeling a life of servanthood is also an important ingredient in the mix.

Have Family Worship Times

There is no better way to destroy the notion that we only worship God at a church event than to regularly band together at home to worship God. Sharing in family worship can provide a rich time of mutual understanding and personal development while also building deeper unity within the family.

Because most Christians struggle to find the presence of God in the congregational church, it behooves you to discover ways to enter into God's presence as a family, finding time, places, and practices that your family finds meaningful. The approach you take need not be a replica of the congregational worship model. If worship is more about attitude and authentic expression than process and tradition, then the means to worship that move you and your family represent an appropriate approach to pursue.

ARMED FOR THE BATTLE

To equip your family as a spiritual center, you must recognize and integrate three simple truths into your efforts.

First, you will not effectively build your family into a spiritual center unless your family becomes a priority in your life. We invest our time, energy, and expertise in those things that we think are worth the investment. People in the thirty-to-fifty age bracket, in particular, position career achievement as more significant than family development. How utterly wrong!

Family is the basic building block of our society; it is the most important set of personal relationships we will experience; it is the core of the Christian community; and it represents the domain in which we are likely to achieve our most significant influence. In the new world of the Church, you and I must think of the family as a major priority.

Second, we are not likely to have much impact on the spiritual development of our families unless we have a plan for maturation. Random experiences and good intentions will result in the same outcome most congregations produce: little discernible growth among those exposed to the variety of activities and programs sponsored by the church.

Our approach must be strategic and intentional. The plan will work best if it incorporates a vision for what we hope to achieve; a strategy for getting there; specific steps we may take to advance toward our vision; and ways of objectively evaluating how well we are doing.

Finally, remember that we are working with people; people need affirmation. As we prod our family into seeking the mind and heart of God, we must provide meaningful rewards to our kinfolk as they advance in their spiritual maturity. Husbands and wives must also reinforce each other's commitment to being spiritual leaders and coaches. In a culture in which there is not likely to be any other source of encouragement to commit to spiritual maturity, and no other source of commendation for progress made toward spiritual growth and wholeness, we must create means of providing positive feedback.

As the Church continues to decentralize, the spiritual development of our families will make or break the vitality of the Christian Church. Whether you are a parent, a child, or part of an extended family, what steps will you take to be the Church?

[FIFTEEN]
PUTTING IT ALL TOGETHER

IF YOU HAVE READ THIS FAR, you have a sense of how thorough and trans-forming the changes will have to be if the Church is going to be restored to health. The Church must learn from the myriad of reform efforts that have fallen short of the mark, sometimes creating problems more substantial than those the program was designed to alleviate.

When a system is radically broken, it is not enough simply to repair the damage; the entire system must be rethought and, perhaps, replaced. Plugging holes in the dike can work for a while, but eventually the entire dike is so weakened and porous that nothing short of an entirely new structure will hold back the surging waters.

Of course, convincing people that radical change is needed and enlisting them as full and active partners can be extremely difficult. Sometimes it takes a cataclysmic condition to bring about such participation. There are times when a compelling vision and inspirational leadership will effect a shift in the thinking or behavior of the people, but the bottom line is this: People do not change without a forceful reason.

The Church has got to find a way to sound just such a wake-up call to its workers who are asleep on the job. We're not talking about a little tinkering here and a patch job there; we're talking about a major rehabilitation project. We're talking revolution!

I do not use the term lightly. In my training as a sociologist I have come to understand that revolutions are very important and special endeavors carried out by people who live for their cause. The passion and vision of revolutionaries touch your life and mine every day. From the Protestant Reformation and the American Revolution to more modern revolutions such as the civil rights movement and the Jesus People movement, your life and mine are still greatly influenced by past revolutions.[1] To state that the Christian Church in America must hope for nothing short of a revolution in thinking and behavior is not hyperbole. It is an intentional statement about the strategic focus we must embrace if the Church is to be a worthy bride of Christ.

Having spent the past several years studying the nature of various revolutions of the last five hundred years in the developed nations of the world, let me give you a brief guided tour of the key lessons that have emerged from my study. The purpose of this review is to further emblazon in your mind the seriousness of the challenge to the Church today, and the type of vision and passion we must have if we are to resuscitate the Church.

CHARACTERISTICS OF EFFECTIVE MOVEMENTS

Revolutions and movements are organized around passion and purpose. A revolution occurs when there is a sufficient intense dissatisfaction to stimulate people to devote themselves with almost blind obedience to a cause. There seem to be three types of movements that are most likely to bring people together: religious movements, social welfare movements, and nationalist movements.

Influential movements and revolutions capitalize upon intense frustration or despair among a group of people. Rather than seeing the existing woes of the Church as a precursor to collapse, why not identify the reasons behind the mounting disappointment with the Church and strive to convert our understanding of and concern for people's unmet spiritual needs into a viable alternative? If we allow our visionary leaders to provide a biblically based, alternative Christian experience that empowers people to know, love, and serve God in authentic and vital ways, millions of purpose-starved Americans will respond. If we blend people's spiritual frustration with a clearly articulated and appealing spiritual alternative, there is incredible potential to ignite widespread, positive life transformation.

If the American church is to be revitalized, it can learn from the successes and failures of past movements. Here are what I perceive to be the hallmarks of successful revolutions—and therefore conditions for us to consider.

Grassroots Effort

Almost every great movement trickles up, not down. The revolution of faith will not be sparked by the institutions and high-profile leaders who publicly represent the Christian Church today. The role of leaders is to cast a vision for a superior future and provide a means to escape the undesirable present conditions. The movement itself will emerge from the inertia of a groundswell of like-minded people who are willing to act upon their dissatisfaction.

Once that determination exists, leaders can effectively give shape and direction to a movement. Using their verbal skills, strategic abilities, and accumulated resources, visionaries may arise to propose a viable answer to the societal spiritual diseases that have upset the potential revolutionaries. *The implication for us is that the second coming of the Church will not be a clergy-driven reformation but a lay-driven explosion of spiritual angst and piety.*

The most effective grassroots efforts are lean, streamlined coalitions. Adding more and more people is not the goal; the existing Church has more than enough people to change the world. The new Church must mobilize people with the appropriate perspective about the content of Christianity and its personal and cultural implications. When this happens, people will respond with an intense desire to be part of this transformational movement of God.

Future Focus

To the revolutionary, all hope lies in the future. The primary goal of every movement is to replace the present reality with a better one. Successful revolutionaries have no reverence for the past or present. When a group is preoccupied with the present, that is the sign it has become institutionalized. The driving issues become territory and survival, rather than purpose and renewal.

It is also imperative that the people involved in a revolution have a certain naiveté about the scope of their undertaking. Successful revolutionaries are always underdogs fighting an uphill battle against seemingly insurmountable odds. What keeps them on target is their internal unity, their devotion to a common vision, strong leadership, and a belief that the future they have envisioned is both possible and preferable.

This description perfectly fits the "Christian revolution." Short of the empowerment of the Holy Spirit, we have no hope of facilitating positive change. And the notion of revolutionizing an entire culture through the faith and example of a cultural remnant is absolutely absurd without a sense of God's centrality in the process.

Unique Doctrine

Revolutionaries are impossible to deter. They have completely bought into their doctrine, and wholeheartedly believe that they are right and their cause is worth dying for. The core of their message is that together the group will find eternal meaning and purpose; apart, there is only anomie and anarchy.

The impression many people have of revolutionaries is that they want things their way and will resist all attempts at the imposition of rules or restrictions. In reality, revolutionary movements generally exhibit well-defined parameters that are tightly controlled. The future they envision is not anarchistic. As Eric Hoffer interprets revolutions, those who participate are more fearful of liberty than they are of persecution.[2]

While the doctrinal statement of each revolutionary movement is unique, they have at least one thing in common: an agreed-upon, tangible, despicable enemy. The value of this focus cannot be overestimated. Having such an opponent enables the group to concentrate its hostility on the enemy.

Imagine the power available to the Church if those who are disenchanted with the existing Church were able to focus their energy and resources on the true Enemy rather than the impostors (such as church structure, ecclesiastical language, theological liberals, and so on). Sharing such a unified perspective would rejuvenate the effort with new energy and sense of purpose.

Sacrificial Lifestyle

The goal of successful movements is not the attainment of personal wealth, it is participation in a worthwhile, transcendent cause. Achieving the end of the movement, then, requires that people make a sacrificial commitment to the cause.

Those pursuing the revolution are expected to streamline their lives so they may focus on that which is meaningful and central to the cause. A simple, rigorous lifestyle is commonly embraced; the denial of worldly pleasures and goals becomes the hallmark of those banded together for the fight.

Visionary Leadership

It may not be the responsibility of a leader to create discontent with existing conditions, but once such discontent is in place, it takes a strong, visionary leader to mold it into a productive force.

The great revolutionary leaders of recent history skillfully employed a combination of force and persuasion to motivate involvement and to direct people's energies. Revolutionary leaders are effective communicators, with artfully turned phrases and vividly painted word pictures. Their charisma enables them to captivate people's attention with revolutionary vision, unilaterally discrediting the creeds, institutions, and individuals that stand in the way of success.

These leaders invariably surround themselves with a small cadre of intensely loyal, zealous, capable, driven peers who form a tightly knit leadership team. Much of the revolutionary activity is delegated to and conceived by members of that team.

Through verbal skill, emotional resonance, and strategic effort, revolutionary leaders blatantly defy that which contradicts their own doctrine, exhorting others to follow suit. Their goals are audacious, and their gifts and skills feed people's hope for a sudden, major change.

Wholehearted Commitment

People do not join movements because they want the spotlight; they join because they want peace of mind. Participants in successful movements and revolutions are anonymous, indistinct, malleable, and interchangeable. The more compliant and obedient they are, the more useful they are to the movement and the greater the chances of success. Loyalty is one of the minimum requirements of a viable revolution. When the people are willing to risk everything that is most important to them in order to support the cause, that movement has hope.

Effective Assimilation

Movements may appear haphazard and sloppy to outsiders—and sometimes to insiders—but movements that achieve their ends develop ways of effectively indoctrinating and incorporating new members. The assimilation process is the glue that holds the entire operation together.

Such a list of attributes can easily fit the Church. Jesus came to establish a family, not a multinational corporation. His ministry was always geared to developing a grassroots outreach that operated in vivid contrast to that of the prevailing religious system. Jesus' focus was to blend present and future together into a startlingly new lifestyle. His doctrinal slant angered every religious group He encountered because it was so unique.

Jesus recruited people who were willing to sell out to God, with no holds barred. Early in His ministry He clearly defined the qualities a Christian should possess to be an effective moral and spiritual revolutionary:

- *Personal righteousness.* The depth of the spiritual humility and maturity of Jesus' followers needed to exceed that of the most righteous religious leaders of the day (Matt. 5:6, 20).

- *Sincerity.* They were to abandon any tools, resources, opportunities, relationships, and experiences that caused them to sin against God or other people (Matt. 5:29–30).

- *Trustworthiness.* They were instructed to make good on their promises, no matter how difficult the task (Matt. 5:31–37).

- *Humility.* Their goal was to be humble, not exalted. Jesus taught that they would achieve greatness only through meekness (Matt. 5:5; 6:1–4). The goal of their existence was not superiority but servanthood (Matt. 5:42, 44; 6:1–4).

- *Love.* Jesus' followers were taught to control their emotions and reactions, returning love for hatred, forgiveness for offense, and acceptance for rejection (Matt. 5:7, 10, 22, 43–48; 6:14–15; 7:1–5).

- *Perseverance.* They were charged not to abandon their calling simply because events went against them, and not to change their goals because those outcomes seemed unattainable (Matt. 6:25–34; 7:13–14).

To Jesus, ministry was about the development of people's character, not about building bigger and better organizations. His interest was in disseminating truth principles, not crafting organizational policies. He measured victory not by the number of seats filled in the synagogue, but by the number of hearts transformed in the marketplace.

Contrast this with the modern Church. In some ways we have turned 180 degrees from the original purpose of the Church. Today people are better able to recite the rules and procedures that govern their local church than they are to quote foundational verses of the Bible. They are more likely to name the location of their denomination's headquarters than to recall the names of the apostles. Christians are better equipped at listing their legal rights as church members than they are at describing their spiritual responsibilities as members of God's kingdom. They are more familiar with the means of filing a lawsuit than they are with the scriptural principles for resolving a dispute among brothers in Christ.

We have created a well-organized institution, which we evaluate according to its administrative competency, ignoring the more significant matters of how effectively it ignites personal transformation and instills a moral conscience. Too often we have substituted grandeur, efficiency, and orderliness for calling, passion, and impact. In its new iteration, the Church must reinvent itself as a movement of believers zealously seeking to infect others with Christ's love and a passion to serve others. The second coming of the Church will be less of a reinvention of Christianity than a return to authentic Christianity in its original form.

WHEN REVOLUTIONS LOSE THEIR EDGE

It is very easy for a movement or revolution to get sidetracked. More often than not, the loss of momentum is due to internal dynamics, not because of external resistance. People get distracted, begin to accept the status quo, or lose their sense of fighting a meaningful battle against a deplorable enemy.

The Bible has foreseen such tendencies and explicitly cautions us to stay focused on the things of God. Think about the parallels between a failed revolution, based upon historical analysis, and an unhealthy church, based upon scriptural teaching.

They Lost Focus

In Revelation 2:1–7 the church in Ephesus is criticized for losing sight of its first love. The Ephesian believers did the right things for the wrong reasons. They lost their passion and perspective. Theirs became an empty, predictable, heartless faith. Their impact for Christ and the joy that they received from their service in His name was minimized because they became distracted.

They Lost Passion

The church in Laodicea is described in Revelation 3:14–22 as a community of believers who had become lukewarm and complacent. Wealthy and comfortable, they lost sight of where those blessings came from, and the related responsibilities. They lost their zeal to fight the status quo because they became the status quo! Their commitment to a moral and spiritual revolution waned as they became the envy of their peers. The seductions of the world overcame the call to obedience.

They Lost Sight of Their Common Enemy

Revelation 2:12–17 discusses the problems in the church in Pergamum. Although they remained true to Christ and did not renounce their faith in Him, they willingly compromised their beliefs to include the ravings of a false prophetess and the teachings of a heretical cult.

This church lost sight of the difference between good and evil, truth and deception, right and wrong. In other words, there was no longer an identifiable enemy to resist. Through their compromises, they and the enemy became one.

Lessons for Today

The American church could be described by all three of these weaknesses. With the blossoming wealth, emerging technology, and general comfort that have become such an integral part of American culture, the notion of a moral and spiritual revolution based on sacrifice, obedience, holiness, and servanthood seems rather unappealing to many.

The enemy no longer seems so ominous. Most of us deny that there is any transcendent enemy, replacing Satan with a series of straw dogs like "mean people," "tough circumstances," and "laziness." While we are vaguely aware of a certain emptiness and dissonance deep inside, we seek to fill it through superficial activities and relationships. Distracted by our material well-being, we have stopped living the revolutionary vision God handed to us, and have simply accepted our situation as the way things should be.

SATISFYING THE FELT NEEDS OF REVOLUTIONARIES

As we prepare true believers to get into the fray and fight the good fight of faith, let me briefly describe what history shows to be the four primary benefits that revolutionaries require in order to sustain their commitment. Although they may live sacrificially and be focused on the future, they are human and have needs like everyone else.

While people join revolutions because they have found the existing system unable to meet their needs, they remain active only as long as the perceived "payback" outweighs the risk and effort involved. If you have any doubt about that, ask any pastor to calculate the number of church members who are active, growing Christians.

Revolutionaries need clear and compelling *ideology*. They must be part of a group that stands for something important and well-defined. They must be able to proudly describe the reason for their discontent and the alternative that their group proposes. Take away their ideology and they are just a group of malcontents; provide them with an articulate alternative and they become productive, if disquieting, citizens.

Participants also need a sense of *identity* within the framework of the revolution. To commit themselves to the action, they need an understanding of why they matter within the group, and what their role is within the aggregate process. They do not need to have a high-profile role; they simply need to feel connected.

Revolutionaries require a personal sense of *intimacy* with others who share their dissatisfaction with the status quo and who are committed to the ends of the revolution. Nobody likes to fight a big battle against the odds by themselves. There is emotional power and security in finding true community. In fact, genuine community is one of the needs that movements satisfy for many of their adherents. Often, it is through such community that the resolve of adherents is strengthened. The absence of community may completely undermine any hope of establishing a revolutionary presence.

Commitment and identity disintegrate without a sense of *impact*. To keep the intensity burning within the revolutionary group, they must see small victories taking place, and observe ways in which the values they represent are having a positive influence upon people. Americans fear being associated with a loser; the movement must regularly give its intimates tangible evidence of progress.

Naturally, the Church in its authentic form can provide these benefits to its people. The Christian faith is perhaps the most well-defined, coherent, defensible ideology known to humankind. God calls us to find our identity through faith in Him, and through our connection to Jesus. Intimacy is available through the communal aspect of the Church. When the Church is truly being the Church, its ability to foster nurturing, deep, loving relationships is unsurpassed. And when the Church is doggedly and strategically fulfilling its biblical mandate, there is no group of people in the world that has as significant an impact on humanity.

A GLIMPSE INTO THE FUTURE

Jesus instructed us not to be anxious about the future, but to serve Him to the best of our ability in the time He gives us. As you reflect on all of the changes, challenges, sacrifices, and opportunities ahead, you have probably tried to envision what the new Church will look like, and the kind of influence it will have in people's lives. That's a healthy thing to do because it shows a commitment to the future and to strategic change, rather than seeking security by maintaining the present.

Nobody, of course, knows exactly how all of the factors we have considered will unfold. But part of creating a compelling vision is to imagine a preferable future and to work backward from that to the present time, noting what it will take to create that superior future. Have you worked through that process?

A different type of mental exercise is to take a more sociological approach and attempt to predict what the culture might be like a decade from now as the changes we have described take shape in reality. Let me offer a few ideas of what might plausibly happen in response to the changes that may well occur if America continues down the track on which it is currently running.

Moral decline. If the churches across America continue to ignore the evolving cultural change, our nation will almost definitely experience moral anarchy. Without the Christian Church's strong spiritual presence, we will see the unabated erosion of the moral and spiritual fiber of the country. Cheating, stealing, and lying will proliferate. Pornography will continue to flourish. Abortion, divorce, and sexual promiscuity will exist at their current levels, or higher, while euthanasia, suicide, and homicides will escalate.

Social decline. Ethnic violence will break out in major metropolitan areas. Public confidence in government leaders will reach new lows, while the media will push the envelope of free speech. Attitudes will become uglier, as people lose their grip on how to handle the frustrations and meaninglessness in their lives.

Loneliness will tear apart millions of Americans as they struggle to develop relationships with depth. As technology works its way deeper into our culture, more people will work from their homes and increasing numbers will have their own businesses. The ultimate effect is an isolated group of people, physically proximate to millions, but emotionally distant from them all.

Spiritual decline. Americans will continue their search for meaning and purpose in life, but the Christian faith will become increasingly less important in that journey. Drugs, Eastern mysticism, spiritual syncretism, and social psychology will replace reading the Bible, praying to God, and striving to worship God as potential solutions to the significance issue. Many will wonder where God is in all of this confusion and suffering. Without the visible evidence of a thriving community of faith, millions will conclude that there is no God.

Public perception will turn even more strongly against us. Evangelism will suffer in the first decade of the new millennium as Christians shrink from the aggressive questioning of the nonbelieving public. Without a visible witness to the contrary, the mass media will continue to portray churches and Christianity negatively, while giving positive affirmation to the new strains of religions and religious leaders competing for America's souls. Christian doctrine will be sliced and diced beyond recognition—and few will know, even fewer will care.

You get the drift. Without a strong, visionary, significant Christian Church, America will suffer some devastating consequences. But there is, of course, an alternative.

IF WE RISE TO THE CHALLENGE . . .

Suppose the Church answers the wake-up call. The portrait would change substantially—not completely, of course, but significantly in some important ways.

Moral resurgence. The moral conscience of the nation would be challenged to consider God's ways. Families would have greater pressure to handle their own spiritual needs, but with the help of an emerging group of ministries attuned to family needs, the chances are good that millions of families would emerge with a stronger commitment to the pursuit of a meaningful faith.

Leadership will emerge. While the professionals in religion would slowly decline in number, literally millions of latent leaders, denied opportunities by the institutional church, will find new spiritual freedom and joy through the application of their leadership gift.

Christian message will regain respect within our communities. If we begin to make the necessary changes in order to meet the real needs of those around us, the media would back off from its incessant criticism of organized Christianity, primarily out of confusion over what to make of the shifting profile of the Christian faith.

When this happens, we will discover that we have been given a window of opportunity to fully utilize newly developed methods to bridge the gap between the saved and the searching—including the rapid expansion of the cyberchurch and the explosion of independent ministry events. This, combined with the decentralization of megachurches and the emergence of alternative church forms and methods, will give us the opportunity we seek to reach the world for Christ.

A Word of Caution

There are real risks associated with this kind of widespread church reform, of course. With the virtual church and the micro-church in full bloom, church leadership will have to find creative ways to ensure that basic spiritual needs of believers are met at all levels.

Unless we develop a way for believers to hold each other accountable and to grow in faith, there will be a widespread outbreak of heresy, syncretism, and apathy. Without these support systems, Bible reading will continue to tumble, while errant religious conversations (based mostly on emotion, assumptions, incomplete information, and errant interpretations) will saturate the marketplace.

No, even if the Church makes the kinds of shifts we have discussed in this book, there are no easy, fast, foolproof solutions. By making radical changes, we may experience modest spiritual gains. Alternatively, we can be assured that by resisting radical methodological changes, the nation and the Church will take a beating.

ARE YOU READY TO RUMBLE?

Do we need a deep, cleansing moral and spiritual revolution in America? You bet we do! But maybe the notion of pursuing Christianity and being labeled a revolutionary is still a bit jarring for you. That's understandable; the protectors of the status quo (and you may be one of them) work hard to portray revolutionaries in a negative light.

But the question you must answer is this: If the purpose of your life is truly to know, love, and serve God with all your heart, mind, soul, and strength, how well does the existing culture foster your purpose? And how helpful is the existing Church in permitting you to accomplish your life goal?

If you perceive American society to be fair, just, compassionate, loving, moral, God-fearing, and Christ-honoring, and the Christian Church to be a primary, positive agent of transformation within that framework, then sit back and enjoy the ride. If you perceive our culture and the Church to be seriously flawed and deficient, and want to be part of the solution rather than an accessory to the problem, then you must embrace the role of a revolutionary and start making good things happen today!

It is not somebody else's responsibility to improve matters. Someday God will ask you to give an account for your time on earth. What report of your commitment to practical, holy, life-transforming service will you be able to give Him?

[N O T E S]

Preface
1. The books referred to are *The Frog in the Kettle*, by George Barna (Ventura, Calif.: Regal Books, 1990) and *The Power of Vision*, by George Barna (Ventura, Calif.: Regal Books, 1992).
2. Your mission or purpose in life may be defined in various ways. No matter how you describe it, though, your life mission will somehow reflect the principles outlined in Deuteronomy 6:5 and Matthew 22:37.

Chapter One
1. These two outcomes are not necessarily mutually exclusive. However, it seems probable that one or the other will be the dominant, if not exclusive, outcome.
2. When I refer to "Christians" I am not speaking about people who call themselves by that name. In my research Christians are defined as people who say they have made a personal commitment to Jesus Christ that is still important in their life today and who claim that after they die they will go to heaven because they have confessed their sins and accepted Jesus Christ as their Savior. I use the terms *Christian* and *born-again Christian* interchangeably.
3. For further information regarding how much Christians resemble non-Christians in their thoughts, words, and deeds, see "The American Witness" in the November/December 1997 issue of *The Barna Report* (Word Ministry Resources: Nashville). In that article I examined 131 different measures of attitudes, behaviors, values, and beliefs and concluded that in the aspects of lifestyle where Christians can have their greatest impact on the lives of non-Christians, there are no visible differences between the two segments.
4. Terminology is often used very loosely within the Christian world, sometimes to our detriment. An example is how we often mistakenly use *renewal* and *revival* interchangeably. In this book, *renewal* will refer to the spiritual development of those who are devoted followers of Jesus Christ. *Revival* will refer to the spiritual awakening of nonbelievers, leading them to become converts of Jesus Christ. In other words, *renewal* relates to the maturing of a believer, while *revival* relates to conversion of nonbelievers. I will not use these words as synonyms.
5. John 8:32.

6. In John 3:16–18 we read that "God so loved the world that He gave His only begotten Son, that whoever believes in Him should not perish but have everlasting life. For God did not send His Son into the world to condemn the world, but that the world through Him might be saved" (NKJV).

7. The promise to remain with us through the good and the bad is found in Hebrews 13:5. We are assured that God will win the battle for people's souls through Jesus' statement to Peter that "on this rock I will build My church and the gates of Hades shall not prevail against it" (Matt. 16:18 NKJV).

Chapter Two

1. For a further discussion of how people's giving habits are changing, read *How to Increase Giving in Your Church*, by George Barna (Ventura, Calif.: Regal Books, 1997).

2. The various statistics mentioned in this section are derived from the semiannual tracking studies conducted by Barna Research among American adults. Every survey is based on responses from a nationwide, representative sample of at least one thousand people. Some of these statistics are drawn from *The Index of Leading Spiritual Indicators* (Dallas: Word Books, 1996). Other, more recent figures are from studies we have conducted since the publication of that book. All of these figures are recent, however, drawn from surveys conducted since 1995.

3. Peter Senge, *The Fifth Discipline* (New York: Doubleday Currency, 1990), 159.

Chapter Three

1. These qualities can be seen in the great leaders of the Bible. For a more detailed description of how God calls leaders and instills His vision in them—and their diligence in its pursuit—see chapter 3 of *Turning Vision into Action*, by George Barna (Ventura, Calif.: Regal Books, 1996). The chapter gives a perspective on the vision God gave to Abraham, Moses, Joshua, Josiah, Nehemiah, Peter, and Paul, and how each individual handled that privilege.

Chapter Four

1. For an extensive discussion of organizational behavior and corporate lifestyles, consult *The Age of Paradox*, by Charles Handy (Cambridge, Mass.: Harvard Business Press, 1994); *Basic Marketing*, by E. Jerome McCarthy (Homewood, Ill.: Irwin Publishing, 1971); and *Fast Cycle Time* by Christopher Meyer (New York: Free Press, 1993).

Chapter Five

1. The concept of contextualization is based on Paul's comments in 1 Corinthians 9:19–23. The principle states that we are to take the truths and principles of our

faith and—without compromising those truths or principles—develop ways of making them understandable and significant to our target audience. The ministries of Jesus and Paul were completely based on this principle. Each time they encountered someone they would strive to understand the person's need and their key cultural realities (for example language, socioeconomic background, religious orientation); and then respond in a manner appropriate to that person.

2. For a more complete discussion of these and other trends, consult "Reading the Future," a ninety-minute audiotape available from Barna Research (1-800-55-BARNA).

3. The term *minority* must be used carefully these days. Minority groups, such as African Americans, represent the majority in many of our largest cities and metropolitan areas. In a growing number of communities it is the Caucasian population which is the minority group. In an even greater number of communities the population has become so diversified that there is no majority segment; every ethnic or racial group is in the minority.

4. Information on wealth comes from a variety of sources. Among those cited here are data from the Census Bureau; information contained in *The Millionaire Next Door*, by Thomas Stanley and William Danko (Atlanta: Longstreet Press, 1996); and *Trends 2000*, by Gerald Celente, (New York: Warner Books, 1997).

5. The federal government measures poverty through the use of a formula based upon the minimal level of living expenses for households, taking into account the number of persons and age of persons in those households. Many social scientists contend that the poverty index significantly underestimates the true cost of living for most people because the formula relies upon outdated assumptions and ignores the higher cost of living in urban areas—where most poor people are located.

6. This statistic is from a survey conducted by Barna Research Group, Ltd., in July 1997. It is discussed in greater length in *Ministering to the Family*, by George Barna (Ventura, Calif.: Issachar Publishing, 1998).

7. The most comprehensive edition of facts on the spiritual state of the nation is contained in *The Index of Leading Spiritual Indicators*, by George Barna (Dallas: Word Books, 1996). The book contains data pertaining to thirteen dimensions of America's current spiritual character and perspectives. Updated information is accessible through *The Barna Report*, a bimonthly newsletter available from Word Ministry Resources, Nashville (1-800-933-9673) and via the Barna Research web site (www.barna.org).

8. I had the opportunity to discuss this trend in greater detail in *Generation Next* (Ventura, Calif.: Regal Books, 1996), based on extensive surveys conducted among the nation's teenage population. Additional insights into the religious and spiritual realities of our young people are found in Josh McDowell's book, *Right from Wrong* (Dallas: Word Books, 1995), based on extensive interviews we conducted with a large nationwide sample of churched teens.

Chapter Six

1. Some social analysts have labeled the youngest group the Millennial generation. They are the segment born from 1984 through 2002. We have tagged them the Mosaic generation for the thinking style they will possess and for the fragmented nature of the experience they will have as they mature. In this book I will not discuss the Mosaic generation in any detail because their values, behaviors, beliefs, and attitudes are still in the formative stage. In fact, roughly one-quarter of that generation has not even been born yet.

2. As you consider the characteristics of people within a given generation—or any data-based population segment, for that matter—please keep in mind that we are working with averages. You will always find some individuals who do not fit the profile of a segment as described by the majority. In ministry, especially, it is important to balance these two resources: a sociological understanding of the reference groups with which an individual is associated, and an experiential comprehension of the individual. It is rare to find one person who is perfectly described by the statistical profiles that emerge from large-scale survey research. However, most people are described at least in part by such information, which then provides a deeper understanding of how that person thinks, perceives, interacts, believes, communicates, and so forth. It is to your disadvantage to write off such insights simply because they do not provide a perfect fit with the individuals you know from the population segment in question; you can learn important truths about those people by understanding their reference groups. Similarly, you would be ill-advised to accept group-level data at face value and ascribe it without customization to everyone within the reference group. Those who are most effective are able to learn from the macro-level data and apply those insights in personal, micro-level ministry.

3. All names have been changed to protect the privacy of those involved.

4. WYSIWYG stands for "What you see is what you get."

Chapter Seven

1. In Deuteronomy 5:6–8 God tells the people of Israel that they must not worship other gods, that He alone is their God. He warned them—and us—not to bow down to other gods or worship them because He is a jealous God who will punish those who worship other deities or idols.

2. For a more extensive discussion of worship, see my book entitled *Worship That Builds the Church* (Ventura, Calif.: Issachar Publishing, 1998); *Worship Evangelism,* by Sally Morgenthaler (Grand Rapids: Zondervan, 1995); and *The Renewal of Sunday Worship,* edited by Robert Webber (Peabody, Mass.: Hendrickson Publishers, 1993).

3. See Matthew 9:37–38 and Luke 10:1–2. Interestingly, Jesus did not send the group out as individuals, but after a time of encouragement and instruction and

prayer, He sent them as teams to share the good news about salvation through grace.

4. There are numerous passages in the Bible that describe the various characteristics of those who give generously to the work of the Church. Some of the most direct verses in this regard are Psalm 37:21; Matthew 23:23–24; Mark 12:41–44; 2 Corinthians 9:6–7, 12–14.

5. This theme is more fully developed in the first chapter of my book *How to Increase Giving in Your Church* (Ventura, Calif.: Regal Books, 1997).

Chapter Eight

1. For Paul's most extensive discussion of spiritual gifts, see 1 Corinthians 12. The gift of leadership is specifically identified in Romans 12:8.

2. See *Spiritual Leadership*, by J. Oswald Sanders (Chicago: Moody Press, 1967).

3. This is a variation of many existing definitions proposed by other students of leadership. This particular statement most closely resembles that of Garry Wills in his excellent book on sociopolitical leadership, *Certain Trumpets* (New York: Simon & Schuster, 1994).

4. In developing this line of thinking I am again indebted to the work of Garry Wills, *Certain Trumpets*, as well as to Charles Handy for his book *Gods of Management* (New York: Oxford University Press, 1995); Lawrence Miller, *Barbarians to Bureaucrats* (New York: Potter Publishers, 1989), and Bill Hybels from his presentation entitled "Discovering and Developing Your Own Leadership Style" (Barrington, Ill.: Willow Creek Association, 1996).

Chapter Nine

1. George Barna, "The American Witness," *The Barna Report*, November/December 1997 (Nashville: Word Ministry Resources).

2. Our research on evangelism has discovered that a primary reason for people making a "decision for Christ" but never becoming true followers of Christ is that churches tend to emphasize either evangelism or discipleship—but rarely both. Many churches, committed to seeing large numbers of individuals choose to identify Jesus as their Savior, focus so much on getting "decisions" that they fail to provide follow-up education, accountability, and encouragement to the new believers. Other churches are so focused on ensuring that people are "in the Word" that they ignore evangelism in favor of simply preaching and teaching biblical principles, seeking "depth not breadth." However, the Bible clearly shows us that there cannot be effective evangelism without significant discipleship, and that discipleship without evangelism leads to a dying and disobedient Church.

3. Research has suggested that on average lectures to a crowd of people result in very limited information retention. One study, originally published in the business newsletter *Communication Briefings,* posits that within twenty minutes of

hearing a message, people forget 40 percent of the content; they lose 60 percent within half a day of the message; and within one week the average listener can recall only 10 percent of what was said. This information is found in *Why Nobody Learns Much of Anything in Church: And How to Fix It,* by Thom and Joani Schultz (Loveland, Colo.: Group Publishing, 1993), 190.

Chapter Eleven
1. These conclusions are based on findings from a series of nationwide surveys, each conducted among one thousand or more adults, completed from 1994 to 1996.
2. The Navigators have produced numerous training materials in the form of books, study guides, and manuals. An overview of the Navigator philosophy of discipleship is provided in *The Lost Art of Disciple Making* by Leroy Eims, (Colorado Springs, Colo.: NavPress, 1978).
3. See *The Lost Art of Disciple Making,* page. 75.
4. Harry Blamires, *The Christian Mind* (Ann Arbor, Mich.: Servant Publications, 1978).

Chapter Twelve
1. See Fred Smith, "Spotting a New Leader," *Leadership* (Fall 1996), 30.
2. The most helpful books I have encountered related to the process of developing leaders are *Learning to Lead,* by Jay Conger (San Francisco: Jossey-Bass, 1992); *The Leadership Challenge,* by James Kouzes and Barry Posner (San Francisco: Jossey-Bass, 1995); *On Becoming A Leader,* by Warren Bennis (Reading, Mass.: Addison-Wesley, 1989); and *Principle-Centered Leadership,* by Stephen Covey (New York: Summit Books, 1991).
3. For an extended discussion of this process, see my book *The Power of Vision* (Ventura, Calif.: Regal Books, 1991).
4. Keep in mind the distinction between a *mission* statement and a *vision* statement. A *mission* statement is a description of the broadest boundaries of ministry. A *vision* statement provides a specific portrait of a preferable future that God has called you to participate in facilitating. For a more detailed discussion of these distinctions, see *The Power of Vision,* by George Barna (Ventura, Calif.: Regal Books, 1992) and *Turning Vision into Action,* by George Barna (Ventura, Calif.: Regal Books, 1996).

Chapter Fourteen
1. If you are interested in some general reading about Christian family development, there are many worthwhile books to consider. A few that I have found to be especially helpful include: *The Strong Family,* Charles Swindoll, 1991, Multnomah Press, Sisters, OR; *The Christian Family,* Larry Christianson, 1970, Bethany Fellowship, Minneapolis, MN; *Solid Answers,* James Dobson, 1997,

Tyndale House, Wheaton, IL; and *The Five Cries of Parents,* Merton Strommen, 1985, Harper & Row, New York.

2. The Bible provides us with much teaching about family. Some of the passages you may wish to consult include: Genesis 1–2; Deuteronomy 6:1–9; Proverbs 3:11–12; 6:20–23; 13:24; 22:6, 15; 23:13–14; 29:15; Matthew 12:46–50; 15:21–28; 18:1–10; 19:1–15; 1 Corinthians 7; Ephesians 5:22–29; 6:14; 1 Thessalonians 2:7–12; and 1 Timothy 5:3–16.

3. For guidance in the identity of such values, consider: Galatians 5:22–23; Exodus 20:1–17; and Matthew 5:1–11. A multitude of books have been written on this topic as well.

Chapter Fifteen

1. Among the revolutionary movements worth studying are the liberation of the Israelites from Egypt, the first century Christian Church, the Crusades, the Puritans, the French Revolution, the Bolshevik Revolution, and the student protest movement of the 1960s.

2. See *The True Believer,* by Eric Hoffer (New York: Harper & Row, 1951), 32.

[BIBLIOGRAPHY]

Adeney, Bernard. *Strange Virtues.* Downers Grove, Ill.: InterVarsity Press, 1995.

Anderson, Leith. *Dying for Change.* Minneapolis: Bethany House Publishers, 1990.

——. *Winning the Values War in a Changing Culture.* Minneapolis: Bethany House Publishers, 1994.

Barber, Lucie. *Teaching Christian Values.* Birmingham: Religious Education Press, 1984.

Barker, Joel. *Future Edge.* New York: William Morrow & Company, 1992.

Barna, George. *Baby Busters.* Chicago: Northfield Press, 1994.

——. *Evangelism That Works.* Ventura, Calif.: Regal Books, 1995.

——. *Generation Next.* Ventura, Calif.: Regal Books, 1995.

——. *The Index of Leading Spiritual Indicators.* Dallas: Word Books, 1996.

——. ed. *Leaders On Leadership.* Ventura, Calif.: Regal Books, 1997.

——. *Ministering to the Family.* Ventura, Calif.: Issachar Publishing, 1998.

——. *The Power of Vision.* Ventura, Calif.: Regal Books, 1992.

——. *Turning Vision into Action.* Ventura, Calif.: Regal Books, 1996.

——. *Worship That Builds the Church.* Ventura, Calif.: Issachar Publishing, 1998.

Bennett, William. *The Index of Leading Cultural Indicators.* New York: Simon & Schuster, 1994.

Bennis, Warren. *On Becoming a Leader.* Reading, Mass.: Addison Wesley, 1989.

Bennis, Warren, and Burt Nanus. *Leaders.* San Francisco: Harper & Row, 1985.

Berger, Peter. *The Sacred Canopy.* New York: Doubleday, 1967.

Berman, Phillip. *The Search for Meaning.* New York: Ballantine, 1990.

Blamires, Harry. *The Christian Mind.* Ann Arbor, Mich.: Servant Publications, 1963.

Bloesch, Donald. *The Essentials of Evangelical Theology.* San Francisco: Harper Collins, 1978.

Bloom, Allan. *The Closing of the American Mind.* New York: Simon & Schuster, 1987.

Boggs, James, and Grace Lee Boggs. *Revolution and Evolution in the Twentieth Century.* New York: Monthly Review Press, 1974.

Brown, Harold O.J. *The Sensate Culture.* Dallas: Word Books, 1996.

Brueggemann, Walter. *The Prophetic Imagination.* Philadelphia: Fortress Press, 1978.

Burns, James MacGregor. *Leadership.* New York: Harper & Row Publishers, 1978.

Campolo, Anthony. *Partly Right.* Dallas: Word Books, 1985.

——. *A Reasonable Faith*. Dallas: Word Books, 1983.

Carson, D.A. and John Woodbridge, eds. *God & Culture*. Grand Rapids: Wm. B. Eerdmans Pub. Co., 1993.

Carter, Stephen. *The Culture of Disbelief*. New York: Basic Books, 1993.

Cetron, Marvin, and Margaret Gayle. *Educational Renaissance*. New York: St. Martin's Press, 1991.

Christianson, Larry. *The Christian Family*. Minneapolis: Bethany House Publishers, 1970.

Clouse, Bonnidell. *Teaching for Moral Growth*. Wheaton, Ill.: Bridge Point Books, 1993.

Clowney, Edmund. *The Church: Contours of Christian Theology*. Downers Grove, Ill.: InterVarsity Press, 1995.

Coles, Robert. *The Call of Service*. Boston: Houghton Mifflin Publishers, 1993.

Collins, James, and Jerry Porras. *Built to Last*. New York: Harper Business, 1994.

Colson, Charles. *Against the Night*. Ann Arbor, Mich.: Servant Publications, 1989.

——. *The Body*. Dallas: Word Books, 1992.

——. *Kingdoms in Conflict*. New York: William Morrow, 1987.

Conger, Jay. *Learning to Lead*. San Francisco: Jossey-Bass Publishers, 1992.

Conner, Daryl. *Managing at the Speed of Change*. New York: Villard Books, 1992.

Covey, Stephen R. *The 7 Habits of Highly Effective People*. New York: Simon & Schuster, 1989.

Dobson, James. *Solid Answers*. Wheaton, Ill.: Tyndale House,1997.

Drucker, Peter. *Managing In a Time of Great Change*. New York: Truman Talley Books, 1995.

Drucker Foundation. *The Leader of the Future*. San Francisco: Jossey Bass Publishers, 1996.

Dulles, Avery. *Models of the Church*. New York: Doubleday, 1974.

Durant, Will, and Ariel Durant. *The Lessons of History*. New York: Simon & Schuster, 1968.

Durkheim, Emile. *The Elementary Forms of Religious Life*. New York: Free Press, 1915.

Edwards, David, and John Stott. *Evangelical Essentials*. Downers Grove, Ill.: InterVarsity Press, 1988.

Eims, Leroy. *The Lost Art of Disciple Making*. Colorado Springs, Colo.: NavPress, 1978.

Fiske, Edward. *Smart Schools, Smart Kids*. New York: Simon & Schuster, 1991.

Ford, Leighton. *Transforming Leadership*. Downers Grove, Ill.: InterVarsity Press, 1991.

Freire, Paulo. *Pedagogy of the Oppressed*. New York: Continuum, 1993.

Gallup, George, and Timothy Jones. *The Saints Among Us*. Ridgefield, Conn.: Morehouse Publishing, 1992.

Gardner, Howard. *Leading Minds: An Anatomy of Leadership*. New York: Basic Books, 1995.

Gates, Bill. *The Road Ahead*. New York, Viking, 1995.

Greeley, Andrew. *The Denominational Society*. Glenview, Ill.: Scott Foresman and Company, 1972.

———. *Religious Change in America.* Cambridge, Mass.: Harvard University Press, 1989.

Greenleaf, Robert. *Servant Leadership.* New York: Paulist Press, 1977.

Gregory, John. *The Seven Laws of Teaching.* Grand Rapids: Baker Book House, 1954.

Hagopian, Mark. *The Phenomenon of Revolution.* New York: Dodd, Mead & Company, 1974.

Hammer, Michael, and James Champy. *Reengineering the Corporation.* New York: Harper Business, 1993.

Hammer, Michael, and Steven Stanton. *The Reengineering Revolution.* New York: Harper Business, 1995.

Handy, Charles. *The Age of Unreason.* Boston: Harvard Business School Press, 1989.

———. *The Empty Raincoat.* London, England: Arrow Business Books, 1994.

———. *Gods of Management.* New York: Oxford University Press, 1995.

Hauerwas, Stanley, ed. *Theology Without Foundations.* Nashville: Abingdon Press, 1994.

Haycock, Ruth. *Encyclopedia of Bible Truths.* Colorado Springs, Colo.: Association of Christian Schools International, 1993.

Hendricks, Howard. *Teaching to Change Lives.* Portland, Oreg.: Multnomah Press, 1987.

Hoekma, David, and Bobby Fong, eds. *Christianity and Culture in the Crossfire.* Grand Rapids: Wm. B. Eerdmans Pub. Co., 1977.

Hoffer, Eric. *The True Believer.* New York: Harper & Row Publishers, 1951.

Holmes, Arthur. *All Truth Is God's Truth.* Grand Rapids: Wm. B. Eerdmans Pub. Co., 1977.

———. *Contours of a World View.* Grand Rapids: Wm. B. Eerdmans Pub. Co., 1983.

———. *Fact, Value and God.* Grand Rapids: Wm. B. Eerdmans Pub. Co., 1997.

———. *Shaping Character.* Grand Rapids: Wm. B. Eerdmans Pub. Co., 1991.

Hunter, George. *Church for the Unchurched.* Nashville: Abingdon Press, 1996.

Hybels, Lynne, and Bill Hybels. *Rediscovering the Church.* Grand Rapids: Zondervan Publishing, 1995.

Kanter, Rosabeth Moss. *When Giants Learn to Dance.* New York: Simon & Schuster, 1989.

Katzenbach, Jon. *Real Change Leaders.* New York: Times Business, 1995.

Kosmin, Barry, and Seymour Lachman. *One Nation Under God.* New York: Harmony Books, 1993.

Kotter, John. *Leading Change.* Cambridge, Mass.: Harvard Business School Press, 1996.

Kouzes, James, and Barry Posner. *The Leadership Challenge.* San Francisco: Jossey-Bass Publishers, 1995.

Larana, Enrique, Hank Johnston, and Joseph Gusfield, eds. *New Social Movements: From Ideology to Identity.* Philadelphia: Temple University Press, 1994.

Leming, Michael, Raymond DeVries, and Brendan Furnish, eds. *The Sociological Perspective: A Value-Committed Introduction.* Grand Rapids: Zondervan Publishing House, 1989.

Lewis, Paul, and Thom Black. *30 Days to a Smart Family.* Grand Rapids: Zondervan Publishing, 1997.

Lewis, Robert. *Real Family Values.* Gresham, Oreg.: Vision House, 1995.

Lovelace, Richard. *Dynamics of Spiritual Life.* Downers Grove, Ill.: InterVarsity Press, 1979.

Markus, Gilbert. *The Radical Tradition.* New York: Doubleday, 1992.

Maxwell, John. *Developing the Leader Within You.* Nashville: Thomas Nelson Publishers, 1993.

McCarthy, E. Jerome. *Basic Marketing.* Homewood, Ill.: Irwin Publishing, 1971.

McCullough, Donald. *The Trivialization of God.* Colorado Springs, Colo.: NavPress, 1995.

McGrath, Alister. *Spirituality in an Age of Change.* Grand Rapids: Zondervan Publishing, 1994.

Mead, Loren. *Transforming Congregations for the Future.* Washington, D.C.: Alban Institute, 1994.

Miller, Lawrence. *Barbarians to Bureaucrats.* New York: Potter Publishers, 1989.

Moberg, David. *The Church as a Social Institution.* Grand Rapids: Baker Book House, 1984.

Morris, Aldon, and Carol Mueller, eds. *Frontiers in Social Movement Theory.* New Haven, Conn.: Yale University Press, 1992.

Mueller, Walter. *Understanding Today's Youth Culture.* Wheaton, Ill.: Tyndale House Publishers, 1994.

Nanus, Burt. *Visionary Leadership.* San Francisco, Calif.: Jossey-Bass Publishers, 1992.

Nevis, Edwin, Joan Lancourt, and Helen Vassallo. *Intentional Revolutions.* San Francisco: Jossey-Bass Publishers, 1996.

Noebel, David. *Understanding the Times.* Eugene, Oreg.: Harvest House Publishers, 1991.

Ogden, Greg. *The New Reformation.* Grand Rapids: Zondervan Publishing, 1990.

Packer, J.I. *Hot Tub Religion.* Wheaton, Ill.: Tyndale House Publishers, 1987.

Pannenberg, Wolfhart. *The Church.* Philadelphia: Westminister Press, 1983.

——. *Christian Spirituality.* Philadelphia: Westminister Press, 1983.

Peters, Tom. *Thriving On Chaos.* New York: Alfred Knopf, 1988.

Piven, Frances Fox, and Richard Clowen. *Poor People's Movements.* New York: Vintage Books, 1977.

Richards, Lawrence, and Clyde Hoeldtke. *A Theology of Church Leadership.* Grand Rapids: Zondervan Publishing, 1980.

Riggs, Charlie. *Learning to Walk with God.* Minneapolis: Worldwide Publications, 1988.

Roberts, Frank. *To All Generations: A Study of Church History.* Grand Rapids: CRC Publications, 1981.

Romanowski, William. *Pop Culture Wars.* Downers Grove, Ill.: InterVarsity Press, 1996.

Roof, Wade, and William McKinney. *American Mainline Religion.* New Brunswick, N.J.: Rutgers University Press, 1987.

Roof, Wade. *A Generation of Seekers.* San Francisco: HarperCollins, 1993.

Roszak, Theodore. *The Making of a Counter Culture.* New York: Doubleday, 1969.

Rylatt, Alastair, and Kevin Lohan. *Creating Training Miracles.* San Francisco: Pfeiffer, 1997.

Salter, Darius. *What Really Matters in Ministry.* Grand Rapids: Baker Book House, 1990.

Sanders, J. Oswald. *Spiritual Leadership.* Chicago: Moody Press, 1967.

Schaeffer, Francis. *A Christian Manifesto.* Wheaton, Ill.: Crossway Books, 1981.

Schaller, Lyle. *Strategies for Change.* Nashville: Abingdon Press, 1993.

Schattschneider, E. E. *The Semisovereign People.* Hinsdale, Ill.: Dryden Press, 1975.

Schultz, Thom, and Joani Schultz. *Why Nobody Learns Much of Anything at Church and How to Fix It.* Loveland, Colo.: Group Publishing, 1993.

Senge, Peter. *The Fifth Discipline.* New York: Doubleday, 1990.

Shawchuck, Norman, and Gustave Rath. *Benchmarks of Quality in the Church.* Nashville: Abingdon Press, 1994.

Sider, Ronald. *One-Sided Christianity?* Grand Rapids: Zondervan Publishing, 1993.

Sjogren, Steve. *Conspiracy of Kindness.* Ann Arbor, Mich.: Servant Publications, 1993.

Smith, Page. *Killing the Spirit.* New York: Penguin Books, 1990.

Sowell, Thomas. *A Conflict of Visions.* New York: Quill/Morrow, 1987.

Stark, Rodney, and Charles Glock. *American Piety.* Berkeley, Calif.: University of California Press, 1968.

Steele, David, and Curtis Thomas. *The Five Points of Calvinism.* Phillipsburg, N.J.: Presbyterian & Reformed Publishing, 1963.

Stott, John. *Authentic Christianity.* Downers Grove, Ill.: InterVarsity Press, 1995.

Strommen, Merton. *The Five Cries of Parents.* New York: Harper & Row, 1985.

Swindoll, Charles. *The Bride.* Grand Rapids: Zondervan Publishing, 1994.

———. *The Strong Family.* Sisters, Oreg.: Multnomah Press, 1991.

Tillapaugh, Frank. *Unleashing the Church.* Ventura, Calif.: Regal Books, 1982.

Tillich, Paul. *Dynamics of Faith.* New York: Harper & Row, 1957.

Toffler, Alvin. *Power Shift.* New York: Bantam Books, 1990.

Treacy, Michael, and Fred Wiersema. *The Discipline of Market Leaders.* Reading, Mass.: Addison Wesley, 1995.

Veith, Gene Edward. *Postmodern Times.* Wheaton, Ill.: Crossway Books, 1994.

Warren, Rick. *The Purpose Driven Church.* Grand Rapids: Zondervan Publishing, 1995.

Wheatley, Margaret. *Leadership and the New Science.* San Francisco: Berrett-Koehler Publishers, 1994.

Wills, Garry. *Certain Trumpets.* New York: Simon & Schuster, 1994.

Wilson, James Q. *On Character.* Washington, D.C.: AEI Press, 1995.

Wood, James, and Maurice Jackson. *Social Movements.* Belmont, Calif.: Wadsworth Publishing, 1982.

You Can't Make Great Strategic Decisions Without Great Strategic Information

[YOU MAKE THE DECISIONS. LET US SUPPLY THE INFORMATION.]

FOR NEARLY TWO DECADES, George Barna and his team at Barna Research have been carefully tracking the relationship between the Church and American culture. Today, Barna Research maintains the most comprehensive database on the spiritual condition of the nation. Let us put our knowledge and research capabilities to work for you.

There are many ways to access the insights we have on hand. Here's how to get the latest information that will help you minister more effectively.

Books, Tapes, etc.

Based on extensive research, Barna Research provides books, videos, audiotapes, and reports designed to help church leaders. Topics addressed cover all facets of ministry, from evangelism, youth ministry, leadership development, and worship to church growth, family ministry, stewardship, and cultural trends. For a current catalogue, or to order any products, call Barna Research at **1-800-55-BARNA.**

Seminars

The day-long seminars for church leaders conducted by Barna Research will challenge your assumptions, inform you about current ministry realities, and stimulate your thinking by describing the "best practices" of effective churches from across the nation. Call us for information about current seminars and upcoming locations.

Newsletter

Through *The Barna Report,* a bi-monthly newsletter, you can get Barna's latest survey results, with commentary and applications. For a sample copy of the newsletter and subscription information, call Word Ministry Resources at 1-800-933-9673.

Custom Research

Through a variety of research methods, Barna Research helps ministries around the world to better understand their opportunities and challenges. Call us to discuss how to get research that will help you become more effective in serving Christ.

For further information about the services and products available from the Barna Research Group, Ltd., call 1-800-55-BARNA; visit our web site (www.barna.org); or write to us at 2487 Ivory Way, Oxnard, CA 93030-6290.

BARNA RESEARCH. STRATEGIC INFORMATION FOR CHURCH LEADERS.

STRATEGY OF
WORLDVIEW 2.5